Earth, Moon, and Stars

Teacher's Guide

Grades 5–8

Skills

Creating and Using Models, Synthesizing, Visualizing, Observing, Communicating, Measuring Angles, Recording, Predicting, Estimating, Averaging, Using Instruments, Drawing Conclusions, Using a Map

Concepts

History of Astronomy, Spherical Earth, Gravity, Moon Phases, Eclipses, Measuring Time, The North Star, Earth's Daily Motion, Constellations, Horizon, Zenith

Themes

Systems & Interactions, Models & Simulations, Stability, Patterns of Change, Evolution, Scale, Structure

Mathematics Strands

Number, Measurement, Pattern, Geometry

Nature of Science and Mathematics

Scientific Community, Interdisciplinary, Cooperative Efforts, Creativity & Constraints, Theory-Based and Testable, Changing Nature of Facts and Theories, Science and Society, Real-Life Applications, Science and Technology

Time

Six 40- to 45-minute sessions, four 20- to 30-minute sessions, six 15-minute sessions

Cary I. Sneider

Great Explorations in Math and Science (GEMS)
Lawrence Hall of Science
University of California, Berkeley

Illustrations
Lisa Haderlie Baker
Carol Bevilacqua
Lisa Klofkorn

Photographs
Cary Sneider

Lawrence Hall of Science,
University of California, Berkeley, CA 94720

Chairman: Glenn T. Seaborg
Director: Marian C. Diamond

Initial support for the origination and publication of the
GEMS series was provided by the A.W. Mellon Foundation
and the Carnegie Corporation of New York. Under a grant
from the National Science Foundation, GEMS Leader's
Workshops have been held across the country. GEMS has also
received support from the McDonnell Douglas Foundation
and the McDonnell Douglas Employees Community Fund,
the Hewlett Packard Company Foundation, and the people at
Chevron USA. GEMS also gratefully acknowledges the
contribution of word processing equipment from Apple
Computer, Inc. This support does not imply responsibility for
statements or views expressed in publications of the GEMS
program. For further information on GEMS leadership
opportunities, or to receive a publication brochure and the
GEMS Network News, please contact GEMS at the address
and phone number below.

International Standard Book Number: 0-924886-05-6

*Visit GEMS
at
www.lhsgems.org*

COMMENTS WELCOME

Great Explorations in Math and Science (GEMS) is
an ongoing curriculum development project.
GEMS guides are revised periodically, to
incorporate teacher comments and new approaches.
We welcome your criticisms, suggestions, helpful
hints, and any anecdotes about your experience
presenting GEMS activities. Your suggestions will
be reviewed each time a GEMS guide is revised.
Please send your comments to:
GEMS Revisions, c/o Lawrence Hall of Science,
University of California, Berkeley, CA 94720.
The phone number is (510) 642-7771.

Great Explorations in Math and Science (GEMS) Program

The Lawrence Hall of Science (LHS) is a public science center on the University of California at Berkeley campus. LHS offers a full program of activities for the public, including workshops and classes, exhibits, films, lectures, and special events. LHS is also a center for teacher education and curriculum research and development.

Over the years, LHS staff have developed a multitude of activities, assembly programs, classes, and interactive exhibits. These programs have proven to be successful at the Hall and should be useful to schools, other science centers, museums, and community groups. A number of these guided-discovery activities have been published under the Great Explorations in Math and Science (GEMS) title, after an extensive refinement process that includes classroom testing of trial versions, modifications to ensure the use of easy-to-obtain materials, and carefully written and edited step-by-step instructions and background information to allow presentation by teachers without special background in mathematics or science.

Staff

Glenn T. Seaborg, *Principal Investigator*
Jacqueline Barber, *Director*
Cary Sneider, *Curriculum Specialist*
Katharine Barrett, Edna DeVore, John Erickson, Jaine Kopp, Kimi Hosoume, Laura Lowell, Linda Lipner, Laura Tucker, Carolyn Willard, *Staff Development Specialists*
Jan M. Goodman, *Mathematics Consultant*
Cynthia Eaton, *Administrative Coordinator*
Karen Milligan, *Distribution Coordinator*
Lisa Haderlie Baker, *Art Director*
Carol Bevilacqua and Lisa Klofkorn, *Designers*
Lincoln Bergman and Kay Fairwell, *Editors*

Contributing Authors

Jacqueline Barber	Jan M. Goodman
Katharine Barrett	Alan Gould
Lincoln Bergman	Kimi Hosoume
Jaine Kopp	Susan Jagoda
Linda Lipner	Larry Malone
Laura Lowell	Cary I. Sneider
Linda De Lucchi	Jennifer Meux White
Jean Echols	Carolyn Willard

Reviewers

We would like to thank the following educators who reviewed, tested, or coordinated the reviewing of GEMS materials in manuscript form. Their critical comments and recommendations contributed significantly to these GEMS publications. Their participation does not necessarily imply endorsement of the GEMS program.

ALASKA
Olyn Garfield*
Galena City School, Galena

ARIZONA
Bill Armistead
Moon Mountain School, Phoenix

Flo-Ann Barwick
Lookout Mountain School, Phoenix

Richard E. Clark*
Washington School District, Phoenix

Bob Heath
Roadrunner School, Phoenix

Edie Helledy
Manzanita School, Phoenix

Greg Jesberger
Maryland School, Phoenix

Mark Kauppila
Acacia School, Phoenix

Karen Lee
Moon Mountain School, Phoenix

George Lewis
John Jacobs School, Phoenix

John Little
Palo Verde School, Phoenix

Tom Lutz
Palo Verde School, Phoenix

Tim Maki
Cactus Wren School, Phoenix

Don Metzler
Moon Mountain School, Phoenix

John O'Daniel
John Jacobs School, Phoenix

Donna Pickering
Orangewood School, Phoenix

Brenda Pierce
Cholla School, Phoenix

Ken Redfield
Washington School, Phoenix

Jean Reinoehl
Alta Vista School, Phoenix

Liz Sandberg
Desert Foothills School, Phoenix

Sandy Stanley
Manzanita School, Phoenix

Charri Strong
Lookout Mountain School, Phoenix

Shirley Vojtko
Cholla School, Phoenix

CALIFORNIA
Bob Alpert*
Vista School, Albany

Karen Ardito
White Hill Junior High School, Fairfax

James Boulier
Dan Mini Elementary School, Vallejo

Susan Butsch
Albany Middle School, Albany

Susan Chan
Cornell School, Albany

Robin Davis
Albany Middle School, Albany

Claudia Hall
Horner Junior High School, Fremont

Dale Kerstad*
Cave Elementary School, Vallejo

Joanna Klaseen
Albany Middle School, Albany

Margaret Lacrampe
Sleepy Hollow School, Orinda

Linda McClanahan*
Horner Junior High School, Fremont

Tina Neivelt
Cave Elementary School, Vallejo

Neil Nelson
Cave Elementary School, Vallejo

Mark Piccillo
Frick Junior High School, Oakland

Cindy Plambeck
Albany Middle School, Albany

Susan Power
Albany Middle School, Albany

Carol Rutherford
Cave Elementary School, Vallejo

Jim Salak
Cave Elementary School, Vallejo

Rich Salisbury
Albany Middle School, Albany

Secondo Sarpieri*
Vallejo City Unified School District, Vallejo

Bob Shogren*
Albany Middle School, Albany

Theodore L. Smith
Frick Junior High School, Oakland

Kay Sorg
Albany Middle School, Albany

Bonnie Square
Cave Elementary School, Vallejo

Jack Thornton*
Dan Mini Elementary School, Vallejo

Alice Tolinder*
Vallejo City Unified School District, Vallejo

Pamela Zimmerman
Cornell School, Albany

KENTUCKY
Mary Artner
Adath Jeshurun Preschool, Louisville

Alice Atchley
Wheatley Elementary School, Louisville

Sandi Babbitz
Adath Jeshurun Preschool, Louisville

Phyl Breuer
Holy Spirit School, Louisville

Toni Davidson
Thomas Jefferson Middle School, Louisville

August Drufke
Museum of History and Science, Louisville

Riva Drutz
Adath Jeshurun Preschool, Louisville

Linda Erman
Adath Jeshurun Preschool, Louisville

Jennie Ewalt
Adath Jeshurun Preschool, Louisville

Sam Foster
Museum of History and Science, Louisville

Nancy Glaser
Thomas Jefferson Middle School, Louisville

Laura Hansen
Sacred Heart Model School, Louisville

Leo Harrison
Thomas Jefferson Middle School, Louisville

Muriel Johnson
Thomas Jefferson Middle School, Louisville

Pam Laveck
Sacred Heart Model School, Louisville

Amy S. Lowen*
Museum of History and Science, Louisville

Theresa H. Mattei*
Museum of History and Science, Louisville

Brad Matthews
Jefferson County Public Schools, Louisville

Cathy Maddox
Thomas Jefferson Middle School, Louisville

Sherrie Morgan
Prelude Preschool, Louisville

Sister Mary Mueller
Sacred Heart Model School, Louisville

Tony Peake
Brown School, Louisville

Ann Peterson
Adath Jeshurun Preschool, Louisville

Mike Plamp
Museum of History and Science, Louisville

John Record
Thomas Jefferson Middle School, Louisville

Susan Reigler
St. Francis High School, Louisville

Anne Renner
Wheatley Elementary School, Louisville

Ken Rosenbaum
Jefferson County Public Schools, Louisville

Edna Schoenbaechler
Museum of History and Science, Louisville

Melissa Shore
Museum of History and Science, Louisville

Joan Stewart
DuPont Manual Magnet School, Louisville

Jenna Stinson
Thomas Jefferson Middle School, Louisville

Dr. William M. Sudduth*
Museum of History and Science, Louisville

Larry Todd
Brown School, Louisville

Harriet Waldman
Adath Jeshurun Preschool, Louisville

Fife Scobie Wicks
Museum of History and Science, Louisville

August Zoeller
Museum of History and Science, Louisville

Doris Zoeller
Museum of History and Science, Louisville

MICHIGAN
Dave Bierenga
South Christian School, Kalamazoo

Edgar Bosch
South Christian School, Kalamazoo

Craig Brueck
Schoolcraft Middle School, Schoolcraft

Joann Dehring
Woodland Elementary School, Portage

Tina Echols
Lincoln Elementary School, Kalamazoo

Barbara Hannaford
Gagie School, Kalamazoo

Dr. Alonzo Hannaford*
Science and Mathematics Education Center
Western Michigan University, Kalamazoo

Rita Hayden*
Science and Mathematics Education Center
Western Michigan University, Kalamazoo

Mary Beth Hunter
Woodland Elementary School, Portage

Ruth James
Portage Central High School, Portage

Dr. Phillip T. Larsen*
Science and Mathematics Education Center
Western Michigan University, Kalamazoo

Gloria Lett*
Kalamazoo Public Schools, Kalamazoo

Roslyn Ludwig
Woodland Elementary School, Portage

David McDill
Harper Creek High School, Battle Creek

Everett McKee
Woodland Elementary School, Portage

Susie Merrill
Gagie School, Kalamazoo

Rick Omilian*
Science and Mathematics Education Center
Western Michigan University, Kalamazoo

Kathy Patton
Northeastern Elementary School, Kalamazoo

Rebecca Penney
Harper Creek High School, Battle Creek

Shirley Pickens
Schoolcraft Elementary School, Schoolcraft

Deb Ply
South Junior High School, Kalamazoo

Sue Schell
Gagie School, Kalamazoo

Sharon Schillaci
Schoolcraft Elementary School, Schoolcraft

Julie Schmidt
Gagie School, Kalamazoo

Joel Schuitema
Woodland Elementary School, Portage

Bev Wrubel
Woodland Elementary School, Portage

NEW YORK

Frances Bargamian
Trinity Elementary School, New Rochelle

Bob Broderick
Trinity Elementary School, New Rochelle

Richard Golden*
Webster Magnet Elementary School, New Rochelle

Tom Mullen
Jefferson Elementary School, New Rochelle

Edna Neita
George M. Davis Elementary School, New Rochelle

Sigrin Newell
Discovery Center, Albany

Eileen Paolicelli
Ward Elementary School, New Rochelle

Dr. John V. Pozzi*
City School District of New Rochelle, New Rochelle

John Russo
Ward Elementary School, New Rochelle

Bruce Seiden
Webster Magnet Elementary School, New Rochelle

David Selleck
Albert Leonard Junior High School, New Rochelle

Tina Sudak
Ward Elementary School, New Rochelle

Julia Taibi
George M. Davis Elementary School, New Rochelle

Rubye Vester
Columbus Elementary School, New Rochelle

Bruce Zeller
Isaac E. Young Junior High School, New Rochelle

NORTH CAROLINA

Jorge Escobar
North Carolina Museum of Life and Science, Durham

Ed Gray
Discovery Place, Charlotte

Sue Griswold
Discovery Place, Charlotte

Mike Jordan
Discovery Place, Charlotte

James D. Keighton*
North Carolina Museum of Life and Science, Durham

Paul Nicholson
North Carolina Museum of Life and Science, Durham

John Paschal
Discovery Place, Charlotte

Cathy Preiss
Discovery Place, Charlotte

Carol Sawyer
Discovery Place, Charlotte

Patricia J. Wainland*
Discovery Place, Charlotte

OHIO

A.M. Sarquis
Miami University, Middletown

OREGON

Christine Bellavita
Judy Cox
David Heil*
Shab Levy
Joanne McKinley
Catherine Mindolovich
Margaret Noone*
Jim Todd
Ann Towsley
Oregon Museum of Science and Industry

Oregon Museum of Science and Industry (OMSI) staff conducted trial tests at the following sites:
Berean Child Care Center, Portland
Grace Collins Memorial Center, Portland
Mary Rieke Talented and Gifted Center, Portland Public School District, Portland
Portland Community Center, Portland
Portland Community College, Portland
St. Vincent De Paul, Child Development Center, Portland
Salem Community School, Salem
Volunteers of America, Child Care Center, Portland

WASHINGTON

David Foss
Stuart Kendall
Dennis Schatz*
William C. Schmitt
David Taylor
Pacific Science Center, Seattle

FINLAND

Sture Björk
Åbo Akademi, Vasa

Arja Raade
Katajanokka Elementary School, Helsinki

Pirjo Tolvanen
Katajanokan Ala-Aste, Helsinki

Gloria Weng*
Katajanokka Elementary School, Helsinki

***Trial test coordinators**

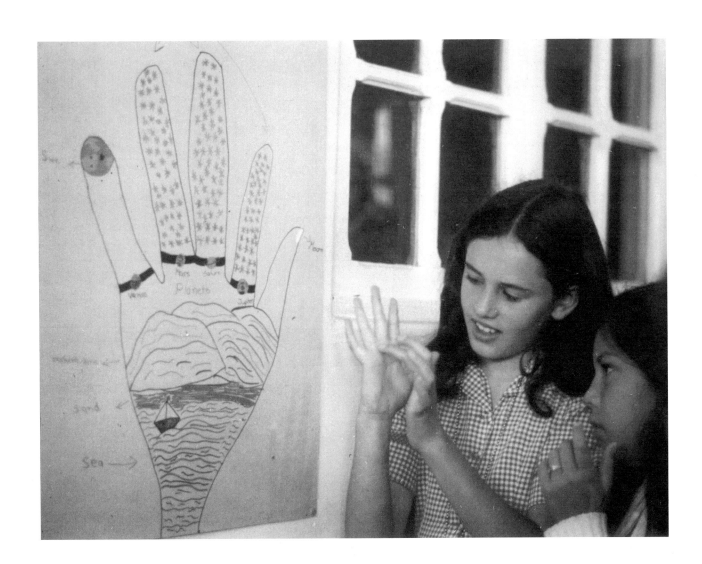

Contents

Acknowledgments viii

Introduction 1

Activity 1: Ancient Models of the World 3

Activity 2: The Earth's Shape and Gravity 9

Activity 3: Observing the Moon 17

Activity 4: Modeling Moon Phases and Eclipses 25

Activity 5: Making a Star Clock 33

Activity 6: Using Star Maps 41

What Did Your Students Learn? 53

Conclusion 55

Literature Connections 56

Assessment Suggestions 63

Summary Outlines 65

Acknowledgments

Activity 1, "Ancient Models of the World," was developed by Cary Sneider at Academica de Costa Rica, a middle school in San Jose, Costa Rica, in 1974. The Ancient Models of the World activity sheet is based on information from *Ancient Cosmologies* by Carmen Blacker and Michael Loewe, London, George Allen and Unwin, Ltd., 1975; and on *The Presocratics*, edited by Philip Wheelwright, Indianapolis, Bobbs-Merrill Educational Publishing, 1960/1977.

Activity 2, "The Earth's Shape and Gravity," evolved from a research study of 185 students from grades two through nine, conducted by Cary Sneider, Steven Pulos, Evangeline Freenor, Betty Templeton, and Joyce Porter. Results of this study are summarized in "Children's Cosmographies: Understanding the Earth's Shape and Gravity," by Cary Sneider and Steven Pulos, in *Science Education*, vol. 67, no. 2, pp. 205-221, 1983.

Activity 3, "Observing the Moon," was inspired by "Where Is the Moon?" in *Elementary Science Study*, St. Louis, Webster Division, McGraw-Hill Book Company, 1968.

Activity 4, "Modeling Moon Phases and Eclipses," is based on an idea suggested independently by Larry Moscotti of the Como Planetarium, St. Paul, Minnesota, and Dennis Schatz of the Pacific Science Center, Seattle, Washington. The Egyptian model of lunar phases is from *Ancient Cosmologies*, as cited above, and the Greek model is described in *Early Greek Astronomy to Aristotle*, by D. R. Dicks, Ithaca, Cornell University Press, 1970.

Activity 5, "Making a Star Clock," is based on a design from *Sky Challenger*, developed by Budd Wentz and Alan Friedman at the Lawrence Hall of Science, 1978, with financial support from the National Science Foundation, Grant #SED 77-18818.

Activity 6, "Using Star Maps," is based on star maps used in the "Constellations Tonight" program, produced at the William K. Holt Planetarium of the Lawrence Hall of Science since 1975, and published in the *Planetarium Educator's Workshop Guide*, by Alan Friedman, Lawrence Lowery, Steven Pulos, Dennis Schatz, and Cary Sneider, International Planetarium Society Special Report, No. 10, 1980, with financial support from the National Science Foundation Grant #SED 77-18387.

The photograph of filamentary nebula on the next page is reproduced with permission of Lick Observatory, University of California, Santa Cruz.

Thanks to Edna DeVore, Alan Gould, Debra Sutter, Greg Steerman, and Carolyn Willard for their assistance in the 1992 revision of this guide, and special thanks to Sue Jagoda for coordinating the revision process. We would also like to thank Joel Blutfield, a teacher in Tucson, Arizona, for his suggestions. Alan Gould and Jan M. Goodman assisted in revisions of the 1994 edition.

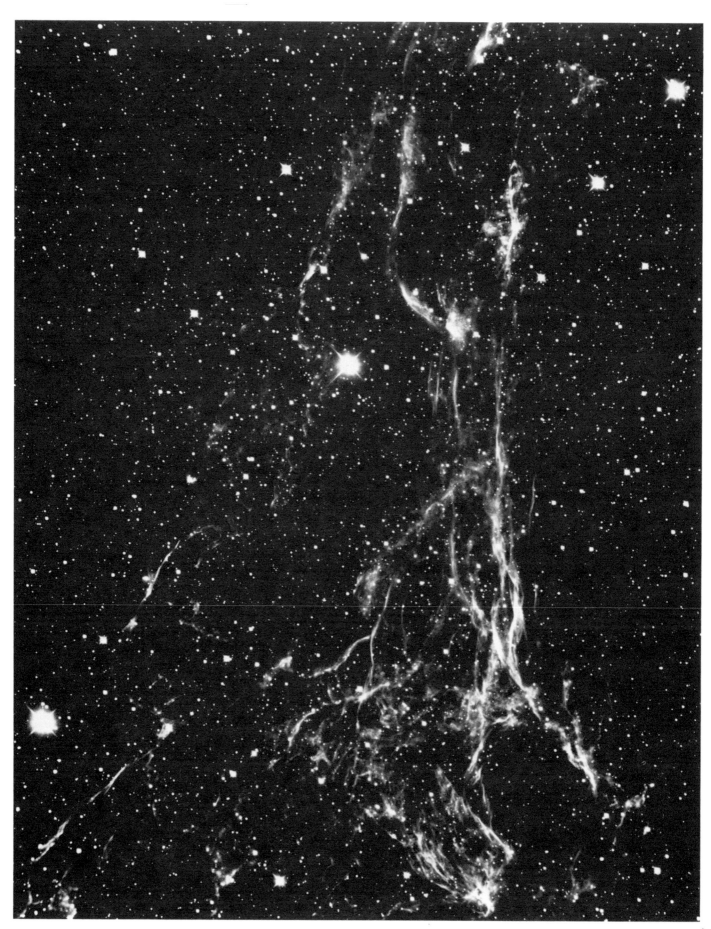

Lick Observatory Photograph

Introduction

An astronomer's laboratory is the sky—and it's right there, on any clear day or night, for your students to learn from and enjoy. The activities in this booklet guide your students in using the sky to:

- answer some of their questions about the Earth, Moon, and stars.

- improve their thinking skills, such as observing, measuring, recording, map reading, using models to explain observations, and inventing their own models.

- gain a deeper understanding and appreciation of the Earth and its relationship to the Sun, the Moon, the stars, and gravity.

To present this unit as effectively as possible, choose a time of year that is likely to yield clear skies. All activities can be done in the classroom or outdoors during the daytime, with a few evening homework assignments. Some teachers have organized evening star parties to help their students with the last two activities. Teachers in some areas have been able to take their students to a planetarium. If you can arrange such a trip for your students, keep in mind that what they see will be far more meaningful if they first have had an opportunity to observe and learn more systematically through the activities presented in this booklet.

The guide also includes an excellent assessment instrument that can help you chart your students' progress in understanding concepts related to the Earth's shape and gravity. See page 53, "What Did Your Students Learn?" for more details.

Several GEMS units make excellent and exciting extensions to Earth, Moon, and Stars. The Real Reasons for Seasons *helps students learn more about the "Sun-Earth Connection," and overcome persistent misconceptions. In* Moons of Jupiter, *students re-create Galileo's observations of Jupiter's moons and go on to tour the moons and create model settlements on them.* Messages from Space: The Solar System and Beyond *ventures into the search for extraterrestrial intelligence as well as the origin of galaxies, the nature of stars, and the conditions that might allow life to evolve elsewhere. And more space science GEMS guides are on the way!*

Two more have arrived! Invisible Universe *and* Living with a Star *have further strengthened the GEMS space science line-up.*

Activity 1: Ancient Models of the World

Introduction

Even from a high mountain, the Earth *looks* flat. So it is natural that most ancient models of the world did not portray the Earth as round.

In this first activity, your students compare four ancient models of the Earth. They learn how each of these models explained common events seen daily in the sky, such as the Sun rising in the east and setting in the west. Your students then invent their own "ancient models" of the world.

The process of creating models leads to a much deeper understanding of how they are used in science than does a model designed by someone else. Your students will learn that the science of astronomy began when people started comparing different models to see which ones were most helpful in explaining what they saw in the sky.

Your students will also learn that these early models of the world evolved from ancient myths, passed on to later generations in stories and art. The parts of this activity which describe and illustrate these myths address learning objectives in language and art, as well as science.

Thales' idea of the world in 500 B.C.
"The earth is like a cork bobbing in the sea."

Time Frame

Part I: Models of the World	40-90 minutes
Part II: Presentations	40-90 minutes

Part I takes about 40-50 minutes if the final drawings are assigned as homework, and closer to 90 minutes if these drawings are completed in class. The length of Part II depends on the number of students in your class, and how much time you allow for each pair of students to present their ideas.

What You Need

For each pair of students:

- ❏ 2 copies of the "Ancient Models of the World" activity sheet (master included, page 7)
- ❏ 1 large sheet of paper or cardboard
- ❏ crayons or magic markers

Getting Ready

Make a copy of the activity sheet for each student and yourself. Familiarize yourself with the models suggested on the activity sheet so you can facilitate the discussion.

An adaptation of this GEMS activity, "Ancient Models of theWorld"
appeared in 1995 National Science and Technology week materials from the
National Science Foundation (NSF), which added an ancient legend
thought to be derived from the Aztec culture of Mexico:

The Earth and sky are two halves of a divided monster that was split in the distant past. The land is surrounded by water. The sky is held up by five trees, one in the center of the earth, and one at each corner. The sky has 13 levels and the Underworld has nine levels. The sun comes out of the Underworld as it rises in the East, travels West over the 13 levels, and is swallowed up by the monster as it sets. It travels through the Underworld, then rises again the next day.

Part I: Models of the World

1. Ask your students to describe the motion of the Sun in the sky. Most students are aware that the Sun rises in the east, goes overhead, then sets in the west. A few students may be aware that the Sun rises and sets farther to the south in the months October through February, and farther to the north in the months April through August.

2. Ask your students, "After the Sun sets in the west, how does it get all the way over to the east before it rises the next morning?" Encourage several answers.

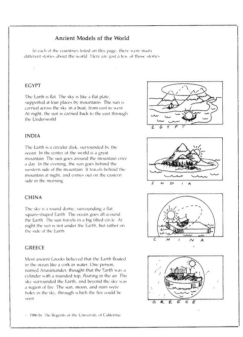

3. Introduce the term *model*, defined as a person's explanation for something that has been observed. Your students' explanations for the motion of the Sun are "models" in this sense of the term.

4. Hand out copies of the "Ancient Models of the World" activity sheet. Tell the students that if they had gone to school 3,000 years ago, they might have been taught that *one* of these models was the *only* way to explain observations of the Sun, Moon, and stars.

5. Ask for student volunteers to read aloud the explanations given for each illustration on the activity sheet. Discuss the different explanations and approaches to the same phenomenon—the daily movement of the Sun from east to west. How might these explanations have evolved? How do the explanations reflect the surroundings of the people who created them? [The Egyptians made flat metal plates, and they lived in a river valley. People from India could not get beyond the steep Himalaya Mountains. The Chinese made beautiful rounded and square bowls from ceramic and metal. The ancient Greeks lived on islands, surrounded by the sea.]

There are many other possible models that could be adapted for this lesson, including stories from Native American and world cultures. Any story that explains or provides a metaphor for the rising and setting of the Sun could be used. The "Literature Connections" section at the end of this guide includes several collections that feature such stories. The GEMS guide Investigating Artifacts has a more extensive list of stories that "explain" natural phenomena, including the movements of the Sun and Moon.

6. Ask the students to imagine that they are living several thousand years ago, on the site where they live now. Challenge them to invent a model of the world to explain how the Sun gets from the western part of the sky back to the east during the night. The model can be a flat Earth or any other shape that might explain the observations. The model can also be designed to explain observations of the Moon and stars.

7. Organize the students into pairs, and hand out scratch paper so they can sketch their ideas. (*Note:* This project can also be done by individuals or small groups.)

8. Give each pair of students a large sheet of white paper or cardboard. Explain that they should draw their ideas of the world so the drawing can be seen by the entire class. Suggest that they label parts of their drawings. If this takes too much time, have the students finish their drawings as homework.

9. When the students finish their drawings, ask them to decide what they will tell their classmates about how their ideas explain the movements of the Sun, Moon, and stars.

Maria and Gina (fifth graders) invented this model and explained, "The people from long ago may have thought that the world was a god's hand. The pointer, middle, and ring fingers were full of stars, and the sun was on the little finger's nail. The moon was on the thumb's nail. The moon would turn back and forth. Sometimes they saw the whole moon or half moon. The planets Venus, Mars, Saturn, and Jupiter were stones on rings. In the morning when the sun came up the three middle fingers would come down and cover the rings."

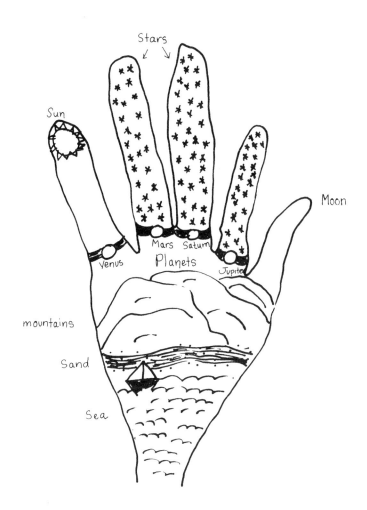

Ancient Models of the World

In each of the countries listed on this page, there were many
different stories about the world. Here are just a few of those stories.

EGYPT

The Earth is flat. The sky is like a flat plate,
supported at four places by mountains. The sun is
carried across the sky in a boat, from east to west.
At night, the sun is carried back to the east through
the Underworld.

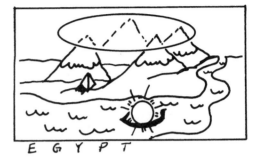

INDIA

The Earth is a circular disk, surrounded by the
ocean. In the center of the world is a great
mountain. The sun goes around the mountain once
a day. In the evening, the sun goes behind the
western side of the mountain. It travels behind the
mountain at night, and comes out on the eastern
side in the morning.

CHINA

The sky is a round dome, surrounding a flat
square-shaped Earth. The ocean goes all around
the Earth. The sun travels in a big tilted circle. At
night the sun is not under the Earth, but rather on
the side of the Earth.

GREECE

Most ancient Greeks believed that the Earth floated
in the ocean like a cork in water. One person,
named Anaximander, thought that the Earth was a
cylinder with a rounded top, floating in the air. The
sky surrounded the Earth, and beyond the sky was
a region of fire. The sun, moon, and stars were
holes in the sky, through which the fire could be
seen.

Part II: Presentations

1. Ask each pair of students to present their ideas. After each presentation, encourage the other students to ask questions. Discuss how well each model explains what we see in the sky.

2. After the student presentations, summarize the lesson by referring to specific examples which show that many different models can be used to explain the same set of observations.

3. You may wish to end the lesson with some additional information about the history of astronomy:

   a. Greece was a center of trade routes, where people from different countries met and exchanged stories about the Earth and sky. Some ancient Greeks listened to these stories and wondered how they could all be true. These people tried to invent models that provided the best explanations for what they saw in the sky. The ball-shaped Earth was one of these ideas, probably suggested by Pythagoras or one of his followers, over 2,500 years ago!

   b. By the time Columbus set sail in 1492, many educated people believed in a ball-shaped Earth. Their biggest disagreement was about its size. Most people thought the Earth was so big that Columbus and his crew would run out of food before they reached land again. In fact, were it not for their unexpected encounter with the Americas, they would have!

The "Mount Nose" activity, described in more detail on page 24, can be done at the beginning of Activity 4, and helps extend and deepen what students have learned in Activity 1 about the rising and setting of the Sun and the ball-shaped Earth.

Activity 2: The Earth's Shape and Gravity

Introduction

Despite the evidence of our senses, we are told as early as the first and second grades that the Earth is really shaped like a ball, that the Earth is round. Perhaps you also remember someone telling you that you could "dig a hole all the way to China," or that people in faraway nations lived "down under your feet, on the other side of the world."

These statements seem unbelievable to us at first, but they are consistent with what we learn in school about the ball-shaped Earth. These early childhood memories provide our first conceptual suggestions about what a ball-shaped Earth implies. As such, they are truly significant learning experiences.

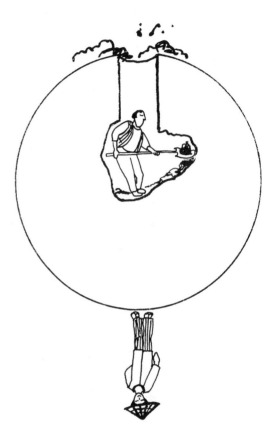

In this activity, a questionnaire launches your students on animated discussions about the implications of the ball-shaped Earth model, which in turn helps lead to a deeper understanding of gravity.

When you lead discussions with your students, please keep in mind that ideas and insights about the Earth's shape and gravity develop gradually. **Getting the "right answer" is not as important as the critical thinking skills that students develop as they struggle to apply their mental models of the Earth to real and imaginary situations.**

Time Frame

Part I: What Are Your Ideas?	30 minutes
Part II: Discussion	40 minutes

What You Need

For the class:
❏ 8 copies of the "What Are Your Ideas About Earth?" questionnaire (master included, page 14)
❏ 8 Earth globes or other large balls
❏ 8 bowls or rolls of tape (to support globes)

For each student:
❏ 1 copy of the "What Are Your Ideas About the Earth?" questionnaire

Getting Ready

1. Copy the questionnaire, making one copy for each student, plus eight additional copies.

2. Borrow eight Earth globes, or obtain beach balls, basketballs, or other large balls to represent the Earth. Remove the globes from their stands, and place them on bowls or rolls of tape, so they will not roll off the tables.

Part I: What Are Your Ideas?

1. Hand out copies of the questionnaire. Ask your students to write their names at the top of their papers and to answer the questions. Allow 10 to 15 minutes for the students to finish. Collect the students' papers so you can look over their ideas later.

2. Organize the class into eight discussion groups of three to five students per group. Explain that each team is to discuss the questions and come to an agreement, if possible, on the best responses.

3. Give each group an Earth globe and one blank questionnaire to use for recording their final answers.

4. Circulate among the groups of students, encouraging them to discuss any disagreements fully and to use the globes to demonstrate their ideas. Groups who agree on the answers early should be instructed to make a list of arguments in support of their answers.

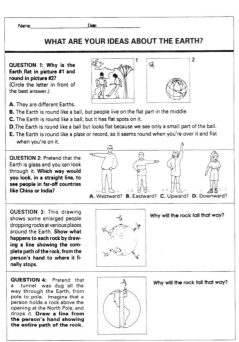

Part II: Discussion

1. Lead the class in a discussion about the questionnaire. Play the role of moderator, requiring each group to support their ideas with arguments or to demonstrate using the Earth globes.

2. After discussing one question, poll the students on the alternative answers. Do not announce the correct answers at this time; students should be encouraged to think for themselves.

3. Following is a description of the kinds of answers you can expect from your students and some suggestions for facilitating the discussion:

Question 1. The correct answer is: "d. The Earth is round like a ball, but looks flat because we see only a small part of it."

You can expect some variation in your students' ideas on this question, since it requires a correct understanding of the part-to-whole relationship between the "flat ground" of our everyday experience, and the "ball-shaped Earth" that we learn about in school. For example, one student thought that the Earth we live on is really flat, and the ball-shaped Earth is "a planet in the sky, where only astronauts go."

Question 2. The correct answer is: "d. Downward."

When first confronted with this question, most people try to imagine which direction they would fly in a plane to get to Australia, and will answer, "eastward" or "westward." Ask your students to imagine that the Earth is made out of glass and that they can look straight through it. You might also use a globe and a ruler to show what happens if you look due east or west: the ruler (representing the way you would look) points off into space.

Question 3. The correct answer shows each rock falling straight down, landing next to the person's feet. It is common for students to show the rocks falling off the Earth, to an absolute down direction in space, or to compromise the two views by showing the rocks falling at an angle.

Question 1.

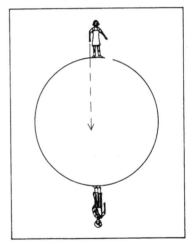

Question 2.

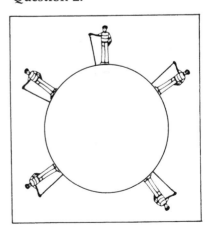

Question 3.

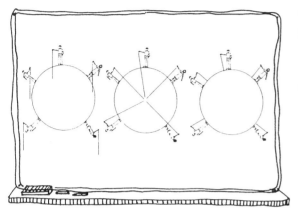

To help the students discuss their answers to this question, draw three or four large circles on the board, each with figures holding rocks as shown on the questionnaire. Invite students to come up to the board to draw their answers. The pictures of three or four alternative views will help you focus the discussion on which answer is best.

At some point in the discussion, you may need to explain why "down" is always toward the center of the Earth. Ask your students to think about the people who live all around the ball-shaped Earth. The only way to explain why these people do not fall off is to imagine that "down" is toward the center of the Earth. To demonstrate this idea, turn an Earth globe so that the South Pole is "up" and ask the students to imagine being there. People on the South Pole must think that people in the Northern Hemisphere live upside-down!

Question 4. This one stumps many adults! The best way to explain what occurs is to explain the history of the concept of *gravity* in this way:

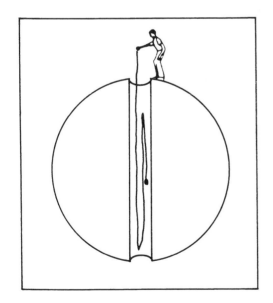

When the ancient Greeks came up with the idea of a ball-shaped Earth, they had to explain why people who lived on the other side of the world didn't fall off. Aristotle, who lived about 2,300 years ago, thought that everything went to its "natural resting place" in the center of the universe, which he believed to be at the center of the Earth. If Aristotle had filled out the questionnaire, he would have drawn a line to the center and stopped there.

The idea was revised "only" about 300 years ago by Isaac Newton, who believed that the rock falls because of a pulling force between every particle within the Earth and every particle within the rock. He named the force *gravity*. From the rock's point of view, "down" is always toward the greater mass of the Earth. Before it reaches the center of the Earth, the rock keeps going faster and faster because it is still falling "down." It only starts slowing after it passes the center, because then the greater mass of the Earth is behind it. If Isaac Newton were to fill out the questionnaire, he would draw the rock falling back and forth between the two poles of the Earth, until air resistance finally slowed it down. Eventually, it would settle in the exact center of the Earth, suspended in the middle of the tunnel.

Again, it is helpful to draw several circles on the board, showing the figure and tunnel in each one. Invite students to come up and draw their answers until several different ideas are represented. Then lead a discussion debating the merits of each idea.

4. After the discussion, give the correct answers, as outlined above, as "the opinion of most scientists."

5. To evaluate this activity, have your students complete the questionnaire again, two or three weeks later.

Research on how students gain understanding of the Earth's shape indicates that the learning process is a gradual one. The questionnaire can be used to construct a class "profile" and determine levels of understanding to help guide appropriate Going Further activities. See pages 53–54 of this guide for suggestions on how to do this.

WHAT ARE YOUR IDEAS ABOUT THE EARTH?

QUESTION 1: Why is the Earth flat in picture #1 and round in picture #2?
(Circle the letter in front of the best answer.)

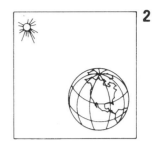

A. They are different Earths.

B. The Earth is round like a ball, but people live on the flat part in the middle.

C. The Earth is round like a ball, but it has flat spots on it.

D. The Earth is round like a ball but looks flat because we see only a small part of the ball.

E. The Earth is round like a plate or record, so it seems round when you're over it and flat when you're on it.

QUESTION 2: Pretend that the Earth is glass and you can look through it. **Which way would you look, in a straight line, to see people in far-off countries like China or India?**

A. Westward? **B.** Eastward? **C.** Upward? **D.** Downward?

QUESTION 3: This drawing shows some enlarged people dropping rocks at various places around the Earth. **Show what happens to each rock by drawing a line showing the complete path of the rock, from the person's hand to where it finally stops.**

Why will the rock fall that way?

QUESTION 4: Pretend that a tunnel was dug all the way through the Earth, from pole to pole. Imagine that a person holds a rock above the opening at the North Pole, and drops it. **Draw a line from the person's hand showing the entire path of the rock.**

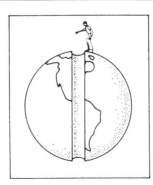

Why will the rock fall that way?

Modified and adapted from the February issue of *Learning 86*, copyright 1986, Springhouse Corporation.

Great Explorations in Math and Science: *Earth, Moon, and Stars*

Activity 3: Observing the Moon

Introduction

When asked why the Moon has different shapes at different times, your students are likely to give a variety of answers. Some commonly expressed ideas are: "clouds are covering the Moon," or "the Earth's shadow is in the way." These ideas are reasonable since clouds do cover the Moon sometimes and the Moon does pass into the shadow of the Earth occasionally. However, they are not correct explanations for the phases of the Moon. Furthermore, students who can explain the reason for the Moon's phases correctly may nevertheless have some difficulty supporting their explanations with evidence.

In this activity your students observe the important clues that made it possible for the first astronomers, over 2,000 years ago, to figure out that phases of the Moon are caused by the Moon's position relative to the Sun. Through their own observations, students come to realize that the lighted portion of the Moon is always on the side facing the Sun. They also observe that the farther the Moon appears from the Sun in the sky, the greater the lighted portion—the crescent phase when the Moon appears closer to the Sun, through full phase, when the Moon appears farthest from the Sun.

Time Frame

Part I:	Measuring in Fists
	one 40-minute session
Part II:	Observing the Moon
	six 15-minute sessions
Part III:	Summarizing the Data
	one 40-minute session

Knowing a few things about the motion of the Sun and Moon in the sky will help you plan times for your class to observe the Moon in the daytime.

1. The Moon, like the Sun, is visible for an *average* of 12 hours per day—sometimes longer, sometimes shorter.

2. The Moon, like the Sun, rises from the eastern horizon and sets toward the western horizon. (The rising point is not necessarily due east; the setting point not necessarily due west.)

3. Because the Moon orbits around the Earth, its position in the sky changes continuously. The Moon moves one full moon diameter every hour, 24 hours a day. Because of this orbital motion, the rising and setting times for the Moon change every day. It can rise and set at any time, day or night!

4. The Moon rises and sets an *average* of 50 minutes *later* each day.

You can use this information to schedule this activity so that the Moon is visible in the sky during the daytime. First, check a newspaper or calendar to find out the date of the next full moon. Also, find out the time of sunrise (within 15 or 20 minutes is fine). Now, make a quick calculation:

1. The full Moon will set in the west just about when the Sun is rising in the east.

2. One day later, the Moon will be higher in the west and set about 50 minutes *after* sunrise.

3. Two days later, the Moon will be higher still and will set about one hour and 40 minutes (100 minutes) *after* sunrise.

4. Three days later, the Moon will set about 2.5 hours (150 minutes) *after* sunrise.

5. And so on...

If your class is going to "measure fists" during the early morning, you may only need to wait three or four days after the full moon to start observing. If your class is going to make measurements in the afternoon, you will need to wait a greater number of days for the Moon to be visible when you go outside. Moon observations do not have to be made at the same time every day, because your students will measure the separation of the Sun and the Moon, not where they are in relation to the horizon.

If you teach science in the late afternoon, you may want to start observations about a week after new moon, instead of a few days after full moon. In that case, you will see the Moon some distance to the east of the Sun during the school day. However, as days pass, the Moon will be visible only in the evening, so students would have to make the observations as homework.

What You Need

For the class:
- ❏ 2 large sheets of butcher paper
- ❏ 1 felt-tipped marker or crayon
- ❏ 1 roll of masking tape

For each student:
- ❏ 1 pencil
- ❏ 10 sheets of paper
- ❏ 1 manila folder
- ❏ 1 calculator (optional)

Getting Ready

1. Just before the first class, go outdoors and find the Moon, to make sure it is not obscured by clouds, trees, or buildings. It will appear as almost full (called a gibbous moon), on the opposite side of the sky from the Sun. If it is cloudy, plan to begin on the next clear day.

2. Make sure you have paper, pencils, and manila folders on hand.

Part I: Measuring in Fists

1. Ask the following questions:

- Did anyone see the Moon this morning?

- If yes, what shape was it?

- Do you think the Moon will be visible tonight? Tomorrow morning?

- If yes, what shape do you think it will be?

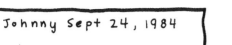

2. Explain to your students that they are about to begin observing the Moon for a month. They will learn the answers to these questions from their own observations.

3. Provide your students with paper, pencils, and manila folders (to use as writing surfaces). Then go outdoors and find the Moon!

4. Gather the students in a spot where they can see the Sun and the Moon. Ask them to describe the shape of the Moon, and to notice which side of the Moon faces toward the Sun.

5. Ask the students to draw the Sun and the Moon just as they appear in the sky. Give them time to complete their drawings, and have them put their names and the date on the paper.

6. Show the students how to measure the distance between the Sun and Moon in "fists" as follows:

 a. Hold one hand over the Sun to shield your eyes. Or, stand in the shadow of a building so the Sun is just barely hidden.

 b. Make the other hand into a fist, and hold your arm out straight.

 c. Hold your fist so the wide part points toward the Sun.

 d. Move your fist toward the Moon one "fist-width" at a time, counting as you go. With practice, your students' measurements of the number of fists between the Sun and Moon will become more consistent.

7. Ask your students to measure the distance between the Sun and the Moon three or four times, until they get about the same number each time. Then quickly poll the entire class to find out how many fists they measured. Help individuals whose measurements differ from the group average by more than three fists.

8. Instruct your students to write the number of fists they measured next to the drawing of the Moon. Then tell the students to put their drawings into their folders.

Part II: Observing the Moon

1. As possible, take your students outdoors every day or every other day to make a new drawing, on a new sheet of paper, of the Sun and Moon. Each drawing should show how the Sun and Moon appear in the sky, the distance between them in fists, and the date. If it is cloudy for a day or two, go out on the next clear day. A total of five or six measurements is adequate.

2. After you return to the classroom following each observation, spend a few minutes discussing how the Moon has changed shape, and its distance from the Sun. Each time, ask the students to notice which side is facing toward and away from the Sun. Ask your students to predict what shape the Moon will be in two or three days, and how many fists from the Sun it will be.

3. You may wish to introduce the terms for the phases of the Moon as they are needed. The phase just after the full moon is called *gibbous*. When the Moon appears as a half disc it is technically called a *quarter moon*, but most students prefer to call it a *half moon*. When it is less than a half disc it is called a *crescent*, and when it disappears from vision altogether it is called a *new moon*.

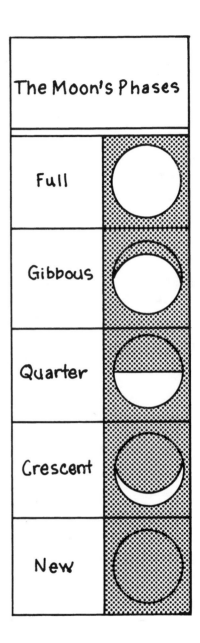

Part III: Summarizing the Data

1. After about ten days, the Moon will no longer be visible during the daytime. That is the time to summarize the observations.

2. Place a large sheet of butcher paper on the wall. Ask your students to take out their folders of moon observations. For the first day's observations, poll the class to find

out the approximate number of fists between the Sun and the Moon on that day. List their answers on the chalkboard, then ask them to estimate the average number of fists for that day. Students in upper elementary and higher grades can work out the exact averages using paper and pencil or calculators.

3. Use a marker to draw the Sun and Moon as they appeared on that date. Write the date and the average number of fists next to the Moon. For each day's observation, add one more image of the Moon, the date, and the number of fists.

4. Ask your students to describe the pattern revealed on the large sheet of paper. Their descriptions should include the following conclusions:

  • Each morning the Moon moves closer to the Sun.

  • As the Moon moves closer to the Sun, its shape appears thinner.

  • The lighted portion of the Moon is always on the side facing the Sun.

5. After your students summarize their observations, ask them to think further about the Moon's cycle by asking them:

  • Where is the Moon now?

  • Why can't we see it any more?

  • When will we be able to see the Moon again?

  • Where will it be?

6. Even if your students have difficulty answering these questions, they have learned enough about the moon's monthly cycle to go on to Activity 4, "Modeling Moon Phases and Eclipses." That activity will help them answer the above questions.

7. (_Optional_): Two or three days after the new moon phase, the Moon will appear as a thin crescent near the setting Sun in the evening. As a homework assignment, have your students watch to see when the Moon first becomes visible. Have them draw the Moon every evening at sunset when possible, marking the date and number of fists between the Sun and Moon. (_Note_: They need only three or four observations on cloudless evenings to draw their conclusions.) Tell your students to add their drawings to their folders. When the Moon is full (about two weeks after the new moon) summarize the observations on a large sheet of butcher paper as you did before. Your students will be able to draw the following conclusions:

- Each evening, the Moon moves away from the Sun.

- As the Moon moves farther from the Sun, its shape appears rounder.

- The lighted portion of the Moon (before it appears full) is always on the side facing the Sun.

Mt. Nose

A Model of Day and Night

Before you do the moon balls activity in this session, but with the lamp already set up, there is a great opportunity to model day and night. This relates to the explanations the students explored in Session 1 and helps students gain understanding through their own direct perceptions.

1. Gather the class in a circle around the lamp. Explain to the students that each of their heads represents the Earth. The light in the center represents the Sun.

2. Ask the students to imagine that their nose is a mountain and that a person lives on the tip of "Mount Nose." With the students facing the lightbulb, ask, "For the person on your Mount Nose, where in the sky is the sun?" [high in the sky, overhead] Ask, "What time of day do you think it is for the person on Mt. Nose?" [around noon]

3. Ask the students to turn to their left, and stop when their right ears are facing the sun. Ask, "For the person on Mount Nose, where in the sky does the sun seem to be? [near the horizon, low in the sky] Ask, "What time of day is it for the person?" [sunset]

4. Have the students continue to turn, stopping when their backs are to the lightbulb. Ask, "What time is it for the person on Mount Nose?" [around midnight] On what part of your head is it daytime? [the back of your head, because it is now facing the sun]

5. Have the students make another quarter turn, so that their left ears face the sun. Where is the sun? [low in the sky, just "coming up"] What time is it? [sunrise] Have the class turn back to face the light.

6. You may want to have students hold their hands to the sides of their heads to form "horizons" The left hand is the "eastern horizon" and the right hand is the "western horizon." Tell the students to turn slowly and watch for "sunrises" from their "left hand/eastern horizon" and sunsets on their "right hand/western horizon."

7. Remind the class of the term model, as someone's explanation for something that has been observed. Scientists today use a model like the one they have just made to explain the way the Sun seems to move in the sky.

Activity 4: Modeling Moon Phases and Eclipses

Introduction

No one knows how the ancient Greeks figured out that moonlight is really reflected sunlight. However, we can imagine that the discovery might have occurred when a curious philosopher noticed that an orange illuminated by a single candle looked like the crescent moon. When he looked at the orange from different angles, it looked like a half, three-quarters, and even a full moon! Using models to explain observations of the Sun, Moon, stars, and other celestial objects has become a cornerstone of modern astronomy.

In this activity your students use a model to explain the Moon's monthly cycle of phases. The students' head will represent the Earth. They hold "moon balls" in their outstretched hands and slowly move them in circles around their heads. With a single lamp, the "sun," lighting up each student's "moon," the students are able to observe moon phases and eclipses. They will then be able to relate this simple model to their earlier observations of the real Moon and Sun in Activity 3, "Observing the Moon."

Time Frame

Part I:	Model Earth, Moon, and Sun	20 minutes
Part II:	Observing Moon Phases	10 minutes
Part III:	Observing Eclipses	10 minutes

What You Need

For the class:
- ❏ 1 lamp with no shade
- ❏ 1 25-foot extension cord
- ❏ 1 40-watt clear lightbulb
- ❏ 1 75-watt clear lightbulb

For each student:
- ❏ 1 two-inch polystyrene ball.
  Note: Styrofoam balls will work if painted with white latex or other water-based paint. Just about any other balls will also work, as long as they are opaque. Polystyrene balls may be purchased inexpensively from a number of sources and are of course supplied in the *Earth, Moon, and Stars* kit from Carolina Biological (see inside front cover of this guide for contact information).

Getting Ready

1. Find a room that you can darken completely by drawing curtains or taping black paper over the windows.

2. Use the extension cord to plug in the lamp. Make sure the cord is long enough for the lamp to be placed in the center of the room. Tape the cord down to the floor for safety.

3. Have a box of balls on hand to give your students. If you use styrofoam balls, the students can stick the balls on the ends of pencils for easy holding.

4. Before class, determine which light bulb is best by placing one of them into the socket and darkening the room. Stand about the same distance from the lamp as the students will stand. Hold a "moon ball" in your hand and move it to one side until you see a crescent. Observe the

contrast between dark and light sides of the ball, then change the bulb and again observe the contrast. Brighter light bulbs usually provide more contrast if you have a large room, or if there is some light coming into the room from outside. Dimmer bulbs will provide greater contrast in smaller rooms with white walls.

Part I: Model Earth, Moon, and Sun

1. Review the results of Activity 3, "Observing the Moon" with your students:

- What are the different shapes or phases of the Moon? [Full, gibbous, half or quarter, crescent, and new.]

- What is the Moon's phase when it is close to the Sun? [A thin crescent, or new moon.]

- Is the lighted side of the Moon away from or toward the Sun ? [Toward the Sun.]

- Optional: How long does it take for the Moon to go from full, to crescent, to new, and back to full again? [One month.] *Note:* If your students did the optional Step #7 on page 23 at the end of Activity 3, they will have recorded a month's cycle.

- Why does the Moon have different phases? [Encourage several answers.]

2. Remind your students of the term *model* by noting that their explanations for phases of the Moon are all models.

3. You may wish to tell your students about the ancient Egyptian's model of moon phases. In the city of Thebes, the Moon was called *Khonsu*, meaning "to travel through a marsh." Imagine a person traveling through a marsh. Clumps of weeds and water plants would block parts of the person from view. This was their model for describing why they sometimes saw only part of the Moon.

Teachers have suggested trying this activity with only half the class at a time. This makes it easier to manage the activity.

There are myths, legends, and stories from all over the world with imaginative and ingenious explanations for the Moon's phases and other astronomical phenomena. A few such books are listed in the "Literature Connections" section on page 56.

The GEMS teacher's guide entitled Investigating Artifacts *includes a more extensive listing of diverse Native American and world myths and stories that explain natural phenomena. In Sessions 3 and 4 of* Investigating Artifacts, *students create myths to explain events in nature, just as they do in Session 1 of* Earth, Moon, and Stars.

4. Explain that about 2,000 years ago, the ancient Greeks invented a model for moon phases that is widely believed today. To demonstrate this model, turn on the lamp, and place it in the center of the room. Darken the room so that the only light comes from the lamp in the center.

5. Arrange your students in a circle around the lamp.

6. Hand out moon balls. If the balls are styrofoam, ask your students to push the balls onto their pencil points so they will have "handles" for holding the moon balls.

7. Explain to your students that each of their heads represents the Earth. The ball represents the Moon. The light in the center represents the Sun.

Part II: Observing Moon Phases

1. Ask your students to hold their moon balls out in front of them, directly in front of the "sun."

2. Instruct the students to move the ball a little to the left until they can see a thin crescent lit up.

3. Look around the room to make sure everyone is holding the ball a little to the left of the sun. The most common error students make is looking at the light and ignoring the "moon." Circulate and help individuals as needed.

4. When everyone can see the crescent, ask: "Is the bright side of your moon facing toward the sun, or away from it? [Toward the sun, just like the real moon.]

5. Tell the students to continue moving their moons around their heads in the same direction, until exactly half of the moon is lit. Ask: "To make the moon appear fuller, does it have to move toward the sun or away from it? [Away from the sun, just like the real moon.]

6. Tell the students to continue moving the moon in a circle until the part they see is fully lit. Explain that to do this, they will have to hold the moon ball just above the shadow of their heads. Ask: "When the moon is full, is it between you and the sun, or on the opposite side of you from the sun?" [It is on the opposite side of you from the sun.]

7. Instruct the students to continue moving the moon in the same direction until it is just half-full again. Ask: "As the moon moves toward the sun, does it appear to get fuller or thinner?" [Thinner.]

8. Finally, tell the students to move their moons so they are very thin crescents. Explain that most of the time the Moon does not pass directly in front of the Sun, but just above or below the Sun. When the Moon is very close to the Sun we cannot see it in the day or night since the Sun is so bright. When the Moon cannot be seen at all, this phase is called the *new moon*. (It is called "new" because it is at the beginning of its cycle. Some ancient peoples thought a brand new moon was being born at this time!)

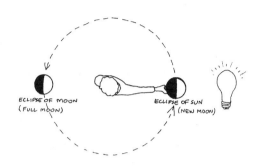

9. Have your students move their moons in circles several times until they fully understand why the Moon goes through phases. The movement of the moon from crescent to full models the two-week period when the Moon is visible in the evening. A full circle represents about a month (more precisely, 29.53 days).

Part III: Observing Eclipses

1. When the students fully understand phases, ask them to move their moons directly in front of the sun to create an eclipse of the sun.

2. While your students observe an eclipse of the sun, tell them: "Hold your moon ball exactly where it is, and glance around the room. Do you see the shadows over everyone's eyes? Remember that your head is the Earth. The people who live where your eyes are see an eclipse of the sun, also called a solar eclipse. But how about the people who live on your chin? Or your ear? [Only the people who live on your eyes can see an eclipse of the sun—the people on your ear or chin can still see the sun!]

3. Instruct your students to move their moon balls around in a circle, as before, until they reach the full phase. This time, tell them to move their moons into the shadow of their heads.

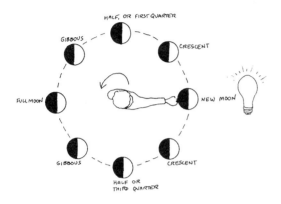

4. While the moons are in the shadow of your students' heads, explain: "This is an eclipse of the moon. Can you see the shape of your hair when the moon moves into eclipse? When there is an eclipse of the real Moon, you can see that the shape of the Earth is round, because it always has a curved shadow."

5. While the students continue to observe the eclipse of the moon, point out that everyone who lives on the side of the Earth facing the Moon can see the Moon in eclipse. But during an eclipse of the Sun, only the people inside the shadow see the Sun being eclipsed.

6. Instruct your students to continue moving their moons around their heads until they again see an eclipse of the sun. Ask: "What phase is the moon in just before or just after an eclipse of the sun?" [Thin crescent or new phase.] Tell them to continue moving their moons in a circle until they see another eclipse of the moon. Ask: "What phase is the moon in just before or just after an eclipse of the moon?" [Full.]

7. Remind the students that it takes one whole month (29.53 days) for the Moon to go around the Earth. During the month there is one time when there *might* be an eclipse of the Moon (at full phase) and one time when there *might* be an eclipse of the Sun (at new moon). An eclipse of the Moon will occur when the Moon passes into the shadow of the Earth where it glows a coppery-red for a few hours. Anyone who lives on the night side of the Earth during an eclipse of the Moon can see it. An eclipse of the Sun occurs when the Moon passes directly between our location on the Earth and the Sun, and lasts only a few minutes! Only the people directly under the shadow can see it. That is why eclipses of the Moon are seen more frequently than eclipses of the Sun.

ECLIPSE OF THE SUN AS SEEN FROM SPACE

ECLIPSE OF THE MOON AS SEEN FROM SPACE

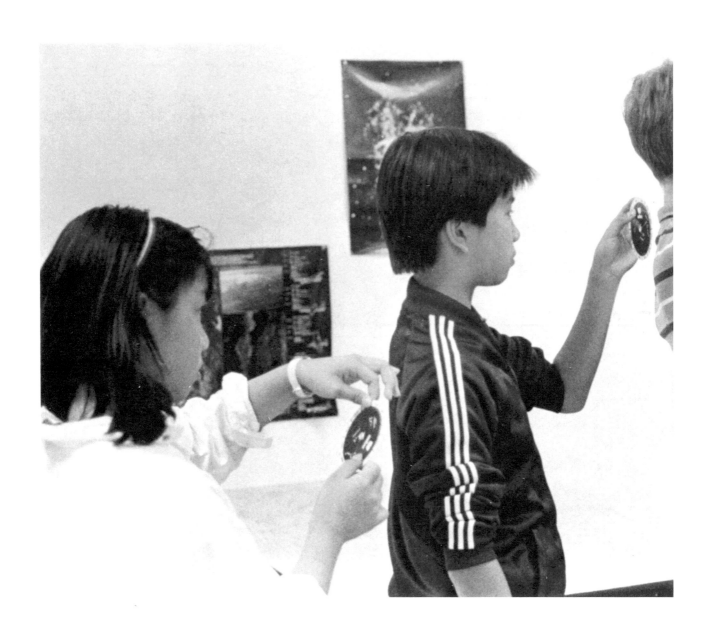

Activity 5: Making a Star Clock

Introduction

Ancient people spent more time gazing at the stars than we do. For one thing, we have television to distract us; for another, the skies are too polluted by light and smog for us to see a spectacular display of constellations. Nevertheless, if your students can find the Big Dipper, they can rediscover the ancient art of telling time by the stars.

In "Making a Star Clock" your students will observe, as people have for thousands of years, that the stars rise in the east and set in the west, and that those stars near the North Star appear to go in circles around it. Nonetheless, even thousands of years of observation can be deceiving, as the great 16th century astronomer Nicolas Copernicus showed. Copernicus postulated that the stars do not really turn around the Earth but only *appear* to do so. He shook the foundations of previous geocentric beliefs, and was met with a storm of opposition, when he suggested that the Earth revolves around the Sun and spins on its axis once a day. Because Earth spins on its axis, the stars *appear* to rise and set. The "Mt. Nose" activity on page 24 provides a related model for the rising and setting of the Sun.

Time Frame

Part I: Making Star Clocks	20 minutes
Part II: Using Star Clocks in Class	20 minutes
Part III: A Spinning Earth	15 minutes

Pick a time for this activity when the Moon will not be full, because the full Moon is so bright that seeing the stars is difficult. On the day you plan to begin, check the morning weather forecast. If cloudy skies are predicted, postpone the activity, since the students will want to use their star clocks as soon as possible. You may want to arrange an evening "star party," so you can help your students with this activity and with Activity 6, "Using Star Maps."

What You Need

For the class:
- ❏ 1 large sheet of black construction paper (16" x 20" or larger)
- ❏ 1 box of large gold stars or round yellow labels
- ❏ 1 box of small gold stars or round yellow labels
- ❏ 1 roll of masking tape
- ❏ 1 meter stick

For each student:
- ❏ 1 copy of the "Instruction Sheet" for making a Star Clock (master included, page 39).
- ❏ 1 paper fastener
- ❏ 1 pair of scissors (If you do not have enough scissors, students can share.)

Getting Ready

1. Make one copy of the "Instruction Sheet" for each student, plus one for yourself.

2. Make one Star Clock, according to the directions on the "Instruction Sheet," to use as a demonstration.

3. Make a Star Clock poster. On a large sheet of black paper, attach stars in the pattern of the Big Dipper, the Little Dipper, and Cassiopeia. As a guide in positioning the stars, use the constellation map on the small circle of the "Instruction Sheet." The Star Clock Poster does not have to be extremely accurate, but the constellations do have to be recognizable. Do **not** draw the dotted lines on the poster.

4. Tape the Star Clock Poster on the wall at the front of your classroom. Use the demonstration Star Clock that you made to position the poster so it shows the stars at 8PM. Do this by turning the inner circle until "8PM" appears in the notch. Hold the Star Clock vertically with the current month at the **top**. Arrange the poster so the stars appear as they do on your Star Clock. Use masking tape to put the poster up so that you can remove the poster, turn it, and re-tape it during class.

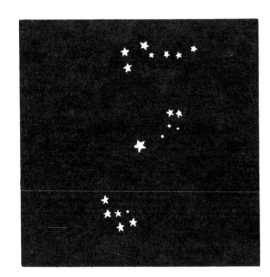

Part 1: Making Star Clocks

1. Introduce this activity by asking your students how people could tell time before clocks were invented. [People used the Sun, dripping water, pouring sand, slow-burning candles, etc.] Explain that a long time ago, people discovered that the stars slowly change position, so they could also use the stars to tell time. After this activity, your students will know how to tell time using the stars.

2. Show the students how to cut out the two circles and the notch in the smaller circle.

3. Then show them how to place the smaller circle on top of the larger one, and insert the fastener through both layers, from the front of the Star Clock. Spread open the fastener on the back.

4. Give an "Instruction Sheet," scissors, and a metal paper fastener to each student. Help individuals as needed.

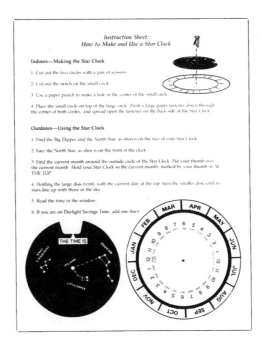

Part II: Using Star Clocks in Class

1. When your students have completed their Star Clocks, focus their attention on the poster at the front of the room.

2. Explain that *constellations* are groups of stars that people have imagined to represent various objects or gods. For example, people imagine the Big Dipper (point to the poster) to be a bowl with a handle that can be used to ladle soup or drinking water. Cassiopeia is supposed to be a queen (some students see it as the queen's crown).

3. Ask your students if they have ever seen these constellations outside at night. Tell them that in order to use the Star Clock, they must be able to find these constellations in the night sky.

4. Ask your students to find the current month around the outside circle of their Star Clocks. Once they find the month, they should put their thumbs on the current month, and hold their Star Clocks so the current month is at the top.

5. Now, ask your students to turn only the smaller circle so that the constellations on the circle look just like the ones on the Star Clock Poster. To help your students adjust their Star Clocks accurately, point out the dotted line drawn from the two Pointer Stars in the Big Dipper to the North Star. Show this imaginary line on the poster by holding a meter stick over the poster. Suggest that the students use this imaginary line in the sky like a hand on a clock.

6. If the current month is at the top, and the inner circle shows the constellations as they appear in the sky, the time can be read in the window where it says "THE TIME IS."

7. Make sure all of your students are reading the same time, within one hour. Help individuals whose times differ from the average by more than one hour.

8. Explain that during the night the stars appear to turn in circles around the North Star. Illustrate by untaping the poster from the wall, rotating it one-quarter turn counter-clockwise, and retaping it to the wall. Ask the students to read the time. [Six hours later than the first reading, or about 1 AM.]

9. Tell the students that they can use their Star Clocks as alarm clocks, by turning the circle so "6AM" appears in the notch. Tell the students to again hold the clock so the current month is at the top and to say "brrring" when the stars appear as they are on the clock. Rotate the poster counter-clockwise, and stop when you hear most of the students' alarms "ring."

10. Once all the students understand how the Star Clock works, challenge them to use the stars in the real sky to tell the time. Suggest that they compare the Star Clock time with the time on a wristwatch. **Important**! If you are on Daylight Savings Time, tell your students to **add** one hour to the time given on the Star Clock.)

11. Urge your students to use their clocks when the stars first come out, and then again just before bedtime, to find out if the Big Dipper really does change its place in the sky during the night. Suggest that they stand near a streetlight, or use a flashlight, to see the Star Clock at night.

Part III: A Spinning Earth

1. The day after a clear evening, when the students have had a chance to use their Star Clocks, ask them to report on their experiences. "Was it difficult? How close was Star Clock time to wristwatch time? Does the Big Dipper really go around the North Star during the night?"

2. Explain that a long time ago, people thought that the sky was a giant ball surrounding the Earth, and that the stars were little points of light attached to the sky. Today we know that the stars are huge balls of fire, just like the Sun, but they appear to be small because they are very far away.

3. To show why the stars seem to go in circles, tell the students to stand up. Then, invite them to imagine that they are each the Earth, and that the ceiling in the room is covered with stars. Now, ask them to slowly turn in place while they look upwards at the ceiling.

4. Ask the students if they can find where the North Star would be in this model. The point directly over their heads will seem to be stationary, while everything else on the ceiling will appear to turn around this point. This demonstrates that the North Star is directly over the North Pole of the Earth. The stars appear to go around the North Star because the Earth turns.

Instruction Sheet:
How to Make and Use a Star Clock

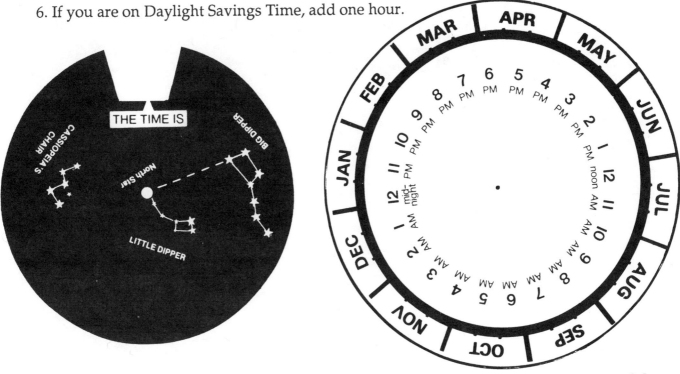

Indoors—Making the Star Clock

1. Cut out the two circles with a pair of scissors.

2. Cut out the notch on the small circle.

3. Place the small circle on top of the large circle. Push a large paper fastener to make a center hole through both circles, and spread open the fastener on the back side of the Star Clock.

Outdoors—Using the Star Clock

1. Find the Big Dipper and the North Star, as shown on the face of your Star Clock.

2. Face the North Star, as shown on the front of the clock.

3. Find the current month around the outside circle of the Star Clock. Put your thumb over the current month. Hold your Star Clock so the current month, marked by your thumb, is AT THE TOP.

4. Holding the large disc firmly with the current date at the top, turn the smaller disc until its stars line up with those in the sky.

5. Read the time in the window.

6. If you are on Daylight Savings Time, add one hour.

Activity 6

Activity 6: Using Star Maps

Introduction

The night sky is a beautiful and bewildering display of stars. To see how the display changes, from hour to hour and night to night, you need to be able to identify the star patterns called constellations. Your students will learn how to find constellations in the night sky by reading star maps.

By teaching your students how to use star maps you will make it possible for them to become familiar with the night sky, to observe its changes, and to better understand the relationship between the Earth and the stars. In later years, the ability to use star maps will help your students find planets, comets, galaxies, and nebulae.

Time Frame

Part I: Using Star Maps	30 minutes
Part II: Changing Stars	20 minutes
Part III: Spinning Earth Revisited	20 minutes

Good conditions for viewing the stars are even more important for this activity than for the previous one. Introduce star maps on a day when it is likely that the evening will be clear and the full Moon is at least a few days away. Many constellations include very faint stars, and it is much more difficult to identify the constellations if the Moon is bright or the sky is cloudy. If possible, plan an evening "star party" to help your students locate all the constellations on the map.

What You Need

For the class:
- ❏ 4 large sheets of black paper or poster board
- ❏ 1 box of large gold stars or round yellow stickers
- ❏ 1 box of small gold stars or round yellow stickers
- ❏ masking tape

For each student:
- ❏ 1 copy of the current star map (see "Getting Ready," page 42)

Note: The star maps in this activity work for the continental United States and other countries in the same latitude. If you are much further north or south, you may wish to make your own maps based on a star finder with interchangeable star wheels for different latitudes, such as *The Night Sky* by David Chandler, sold by Sky Publishing Corporation, 49-50-51 Bay State Road, Cambridge, MA 02138.

Getting Ready

1. On a clear evening before presenting this unit, select the current star map, and read the directions for its use on the following pages. (Each of the six star maps in this activity remain current for the two months marked at the top.) Then, go outdoors to see which constellations you can find most easily.

2. Have the poster from the previous activity showing the Big Dipper, the Little Dipper, and the North Star (Polaris); and make three others showing constellations that are close to the horizon. Use black paper or poster board, and gold stars. (Use large and small dots or gold stars to represent brighter or dimmer stars in the sky.) Do **not** write the names of the constellations or draw the dotted lines between the stars—the pattern of stars on your posters should resemble as much as possible their appearance in the night sky.

3. Tape the posters of constellations to the walls of your classroom, using the star map as a guide. Tape the Big Dipper poster on the wall in the front of your classroom. Place southern constellations on the back wall, eastern constellations on the right (when facing the front of the room), and western constellations on the left.

4. Make one copy of the current star map for each student.

Part I: Using Star Maps

1. Focus your students' attention on the poster of the Big Dipper and the North Star. If your students have done Activity 5, "Making a Star Clock," ask them the name of the constellation. (If the students have not done the activity, explain that the constellation is called the Big Dipper.) Invite a student to point out the handle and the bowl of the Big Dipper. Also, ask her to show how the two pointer stars at the end of the Big Dipper's bowl point toward the North Star.

2. Explain that the ancient Romans called this same constellation *Ursa Major*, which meant "Big Bear" in their language, Latin. Invite the students to imagine this group stars as a giant bear in the sky.

3. Explain that the North Star is over the North Pole of the Earth. So, when you face the North Star you are facing north. Ask the students: "Which way is south?" [Behind you.] "East?" [To the right.] "West?" [To the left.] To help the students remember these directions, you can suggest that they imagine they are standing on a big compass face, or a big map of the United States, with north pointing ahead, east to the right, west to the left, and south to the rear.

4. Give each student one current star map. Explain that the names of the constellations shown on the maps were created about 2,000 years ago. To avoid confusion when talking about a particular part of the sky, astronomers all over the world have agreed to call the constellations by these names.

5. Explain how to use a star map:

> a. First pick the constellation you want to find. For example, find *Ursa Minor* (the Little Dipper) on your star maps.

> b. The map locates the constellation in the sky. Constellations in the center of the circle are high in the sky, near the *zenith* (the part of the sky that is directly overhead). Constellations near the edge of the circle are low in the sky, near the *horizon* (the line where the land meets the sky). Where should we look to see the Little Dipper? (North, or a little to the east or west, depending on the season.)

Interestingly, many other cultures also see this constellation as a bear. If you have time, you may want to share the Native American story on page 44 "The Bear in the Oak Tree Forest," that originated with the Wasco tribe of the Pacific Northwest.

c. The map also provides information that tells you which direction to face in order to see a constellation. Is *Ursa Major* closest to the part of the circle that says northern, southern, eastern, or western horizon? [Your students will notice that *Ursa Major* is closest to the northern horizon.] That means we must face north in order to see *Ursa Major*.

d. What constellation in the real sky must we locate in order to determine direction? [The Big Dipper and the North Star.] So, in order to find any constellation, you must first use the Big Dipper and North Star to determine "north" and thus the other directions.

e. Now, to find the constellation, **hold the map so the direction you are facing appears on the bottom of the page.** Look in the sky to see the pattern of stars shown on the bottom half of the map.

The Bear in the Oak Tree Forest

Long ago there was a great oak forest that was enchanted and magical, because every night at midnight the trees in this forest would move around and visit each other. One day a bear wandered into this forest and got so lost, he couldn't find his way out. He became frightened, and when midnight came, he was terrified to find the trees moving about. The poor bear started racing madly all over and bumping into trees right and left. The trees did not appreciate this intruder at all, and one tree was so upset that it started chasing the bear. Because bears generally are faster than trees, this chase lasted almost till dawn. The tree knew that he and all the other trees had to go back to their original places by dawn, or the Sun would notice that they had moved. So the tree, just at twilight, made one last grasp at the bear with its longest branch and just barely caught the bear by the tail. Then the tree swung the bear up into the sky where we see him now. That is why his tail is so long.

---

5. Test your students' understanding by challenging them to find the other three constellations that you have placed around the room, one at a time. Use the following procedure:

    a. Select one of the constellations for which you have made a poster, and tell the students that they are going to locate that constellation in the "sky."

    b. Ask them to look at their star maps to see if the constellation is high overhead or near the horizon.

    c. Ask what direction they should face to see that constellation.

    d. Tell them to face in that direction and find the constellation.

    e. Do the same for the other two constellations.

6. Invite your students to take their maps home and find as many constellations as possible in the real night sky. Suggest that they stand near a streetlight or use a flashlight to see the star map at night.

Part II: Changing Stars

1. The day after a clear evening, when the students have had an opportunity to use their star maps, ask about their experiences: "Which constellations did you find? Was it hard or easy?"

2. Urge your students to use their star maps again when the stars are just coming out. They should find at least one constellation near the eastern horizon and one near the western horizon.

3. Then, just before bedtime, they should go outside again to see if those constellations have moved.

4. If your students have done Activity 5, "Making a Star Clock," ask them to recall how the stars near the North Star changed during the night. Ask them to predict how the constellations in the eastern and western parts of the sky will change. Then, have them observe and find out. [Stars in the east will rise, stars in the west will set, and stars in the north will circle the North Star.]

Part III: Spinning Earth Revisited

1. Ask the students if they were able to observe constellations in the east and west, and if the constellations moved later in the evening. [Those in the east rise in the sky, and those in the west get lower, or sink below the horizon.]

2. As in Activity 5, "Making a Star Clock," have your students stand and imagine that they are each the Earth, and that all of the people and objects in the room are the constellations. Instruct them to slowly turn in place and look straight ahead. They will see new objects (stars) move into view on one side, go across their line of vision, and go out of view on the other side.

3. To recall how the stars move near the North Star, they can again look overhead as they slowly turn, and see everything appearing to go around a single point in the ceiling.

Evening Star Map for January - February

9 - 10 PM

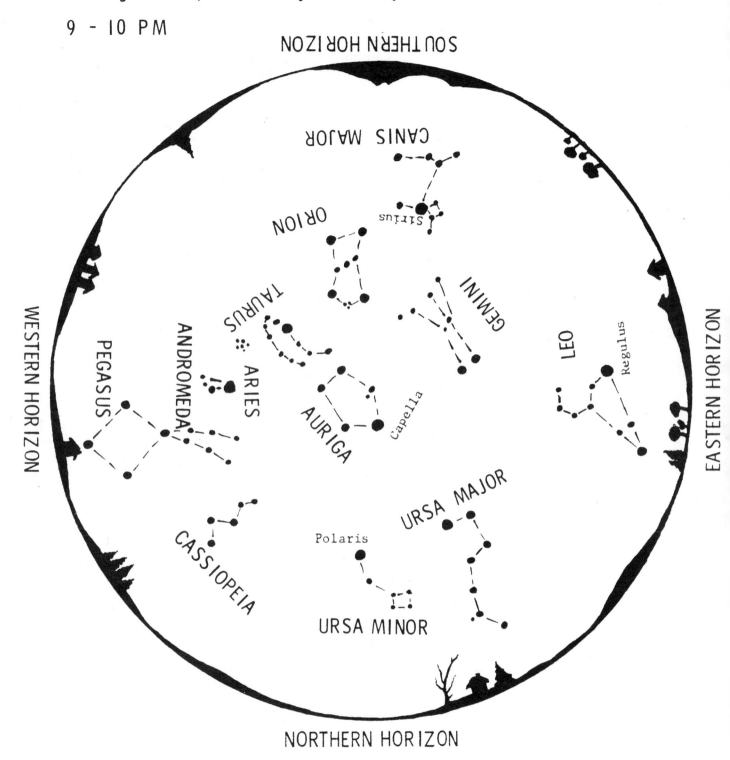

to use map:

Hold this sheet in front of you. Turn the map so the direction you are facing is on the bottom. The constellations in the sky will match the constellations on the map.

Holt Planetarium, Lawrence Hall of Science, Berkeley, CA. 94720.
© 1978, Regents of the University of California.

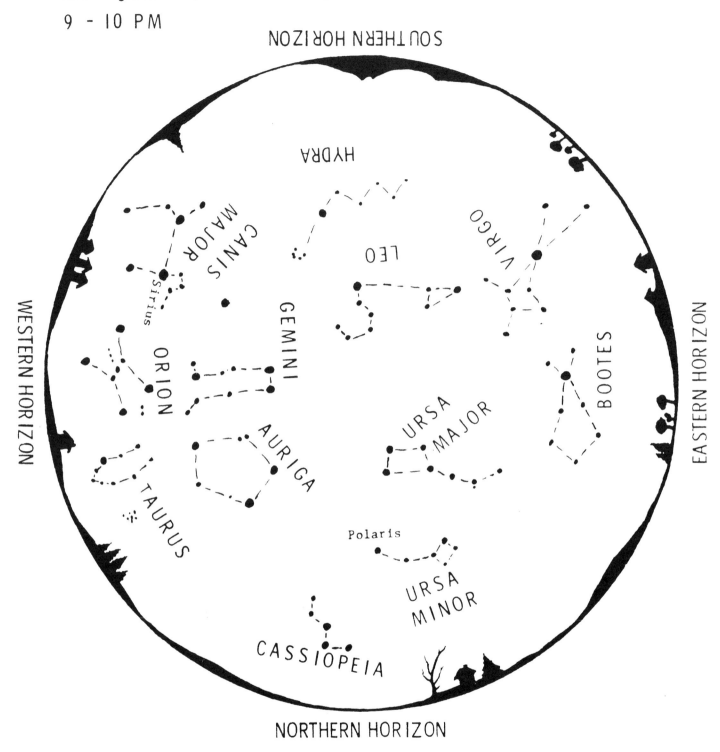

to use map:

Hold this sheet in front of you. Turn the map so the direction
you are facing is on the bottom. The constellations in the sky
will match the constellations on the map.

Holt Planetarium, Lawrence Hall of Science, Berkeley, CA. 94720.
© 1978, Regents of the University of California.

Evening Star Map for May – June

9 - 10 PM

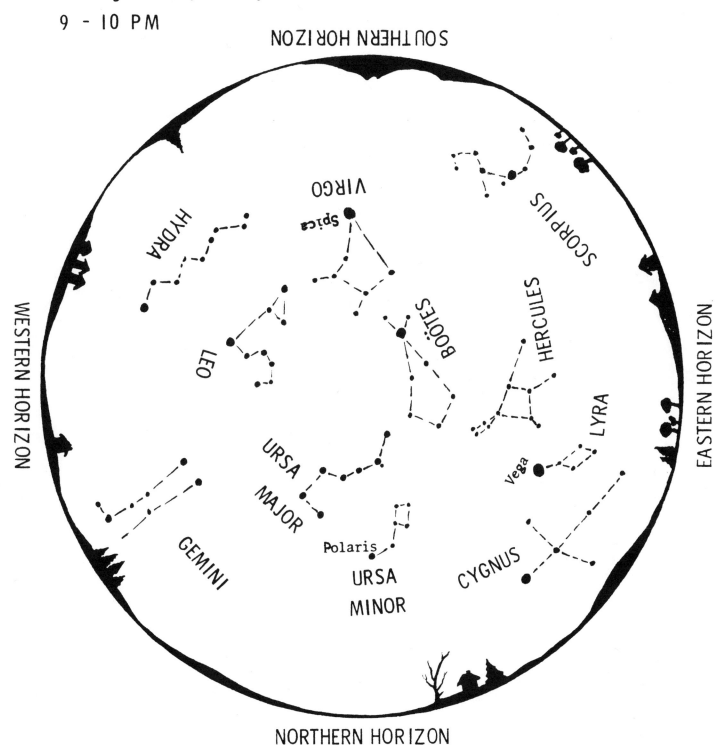

to use map:

Hold this sheet in front of you. Turn the map so the direction you are facing is on the bottom. The constellations in the sky will match the constellations on the map.

Holt Planetarium, Lawrence Hall of Science, Berkeley, CA. 94720.
© 1978, Regents of the University of California.

Activity 6 49

Evening Star Map for July – August

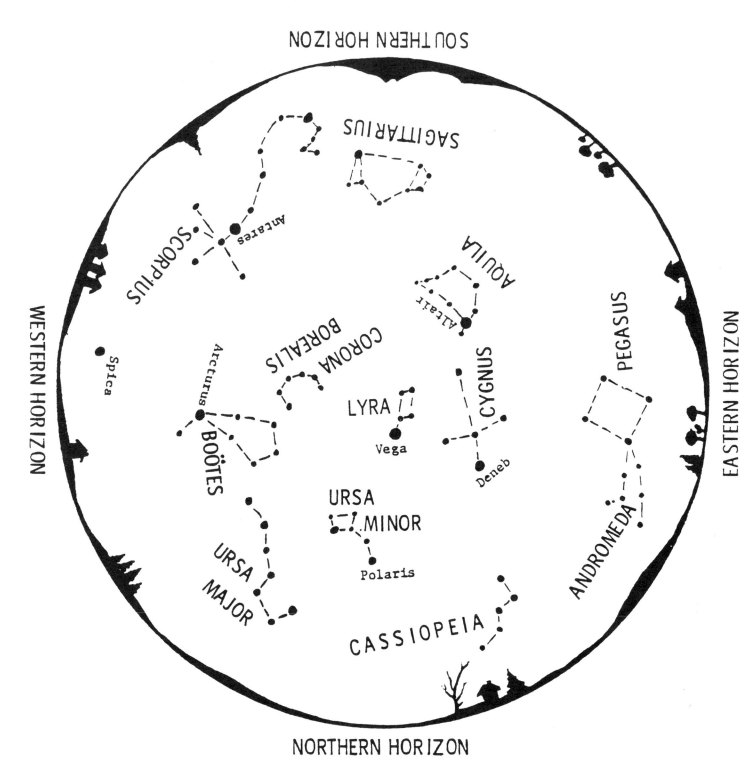

to use map:

Hold this sheet in front of you. Turn the map so the direction
you are facing is on the bottom. The constellations in the sky
will match the constellations on the map.

Holt Planetarium, Lawrence Hall of Science, Berkeley, CA. 94720.
© 1978, Regents of the University of California.

Evening Star Map for September – October

9 - 10 PM

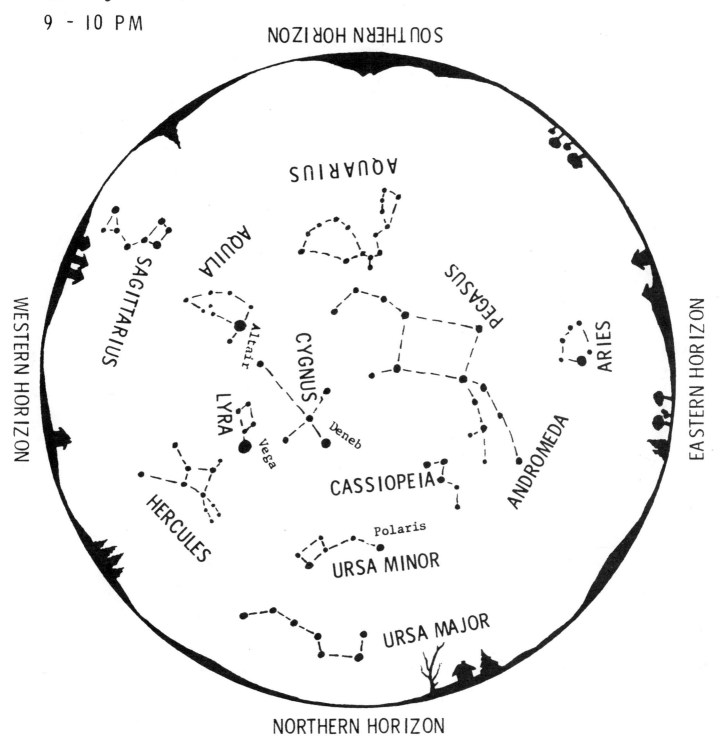

to use map:

Hold this sheet in front of you. Turn the map so the direction you are facing is on the bottom. The constellations in the sky will match the constellations on the map.

Holt Planetarium, Lawrence Hall of Science, Berkeley, CA. 94720.
© 1978, Regents of the University of California.

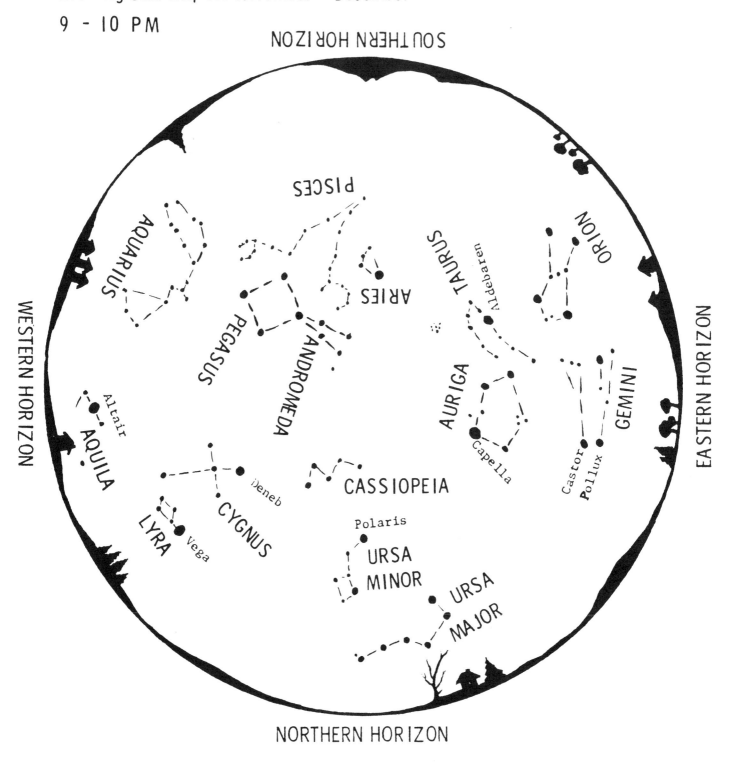

to use map:

Hold this sheet in front of you. Turn the map so the direction you are facing is on the bottom. The constellations in the sky will match the constellations on the map.

Holt Planetarium, Lawrence Hall of Science, Berkeley, CA. 94720.
© 1978, Regents of the University of California.

What Did Your Students Learn?

Many concepts are presented in this unit. Two of these important ideas concern the Earth's shape and gravity. You can determine how much your students learned if you save their questionnaires about these concepts from Activity 2. (See page 14.)

Make two copies of the opposite page entitled "Levels of Understanding About the Earth's Shape and Gravity." On the first copy create a profile of your students' ideas before the unit. Administer the same questionnaire again after the unit. Use the second sheet to create a profile of their ideas after doing these activities.

To create a profile of your students' ideas, use the information on the next page to score each questionnaire on the Earth's shape concept and on the Gravity concept. Use the histograms to plot the scores of your students on these two concepts.

Please do not be disappointed if your students do not all advance to higher levels of understanding right away! Learning that the Earth beneath our feet is really a huge ball in space is not an easy concept; and many people learn this gradually after many experiences like those in the *Earth, Moon, and Stars* unit. Our understanding continues to deepen over time. You can feel very proud if the class profile has shown some movement from lower to higher levels of thinking on these two concepts.

Levels of Understanding About the Earth's Shape and Gravity

EARTH'S SHAPE		Definition of each level	How to classify answers	Number of students
	SHAPE LEVEL 4	The Earth is shaped like a ball, and people live all around the ball.	**QUESTION 1:** Answer D and **QUESTION 2:** Answer D.	
	SHAPE LEVEL 3	The Earth is shaped like a ball, but people live just on top of the ball.	**QUESTION 1:** Answer D and **QUESTION 2:** Answers A, B, or C.	
	SHAPE LEVEL 2	The Earth is shaped like a ball, but people live on the flat parts of it (or inside the ball).	**QUESTION 1:** Either answer B or C.	
	SHAPE LEVEL 1	The Earth is flat.	**QUESTION 1:** Either Answer A or E, or no answer at all.	

GRAVITY		Definition of each level	How to classify answers	Number of students
	GRAVITY LEVEL 3	Objects fall toward the *center* of the Earth.	**QUESTION 3:** Rocks are shown falling straight down to the surface of the Earth, near each figure's feet, and **QUESTION 4:** The rock is shown falling toward the Earth's center, where it either falls through and bobs up and down, or stops in the center.	
	GRAVITY LEVEL 2	Objects fall toward the *surface* of the Earth.	**QUESTION 3:** Rocks are shown falling straight down to the surface of the Earth, near each figure's feet, and **QUESTION 4:** The rocks do not end up in the Earth's center. (They may be shown passing all the way through the earth, sticking to the Earth's surface, or taking some other path.)	
	GRAVITY LEVEL 1	Objects fall *down* in space.	**QUESTION 3:** Rocks are *not* shown falling straight down to the surface of the Earth. (They may be falling down to the bottom of the page or shooting at some other angle around the planet.)	

CLASS PROFILE—EARTH'S SHAPE

LEVEL 1 LEVEL 2 LEVEL 3 LEVEL 4

NUMBER OF STUDENTS: 30, 28, 26, 24, 22, 20, 18, 16, 14, 12, 10, 8, 6, 4, 2, 0

GRAVITY

LEVEL 1 LEVEL 2 LEVEL 3

NUMBER OF STUDENTS: 30, 28, 26, 24, 22, 20, 18, 16, 14, 12, 10, 8, 6, 4, 2, 0

Conclusion

All of the activities in *Earth, Moon, and Stars* are designed to provide your students with a good basic framework for comprehending the ball-shaped object on which we live, and its relation to the infinite reaches of the universe. The use of models in many of these activities helps provide students with new ways of understanding phenomena and analyzing problems, in addition to being one of the best ways to convey astronomical concepts. The sense of scientific history embodied in ancient models and myths helps students understand that human knowledge is relative and always in the process of change, that even our own seemingly advanced theories will be modified by the discoveries of the future.

We live in an age when the human species has been able to voyage into outer space, walk on the Moon, land exploratory craft on other planets, and process information from distant galaxies by means of new technologies. This constantly expanding contact makes a clear and stimulating introduction to astronomy an invaluable asset to students of all ages. It is our hope that *Earth, Moon, and Stars* will help serve as such an introduction for your students.

Literature Connections

Books that explain the physical world through myths and legends are a perfect accompaniment to Session 1 of the guide, in which students create their own myths or models to explain the Sun's apparent movement. Of course, certain myths and legends can also be matched with other sessions of the guide. For instance, legends about the Moon or stars can be connected to the class sessions on moon phases or constellations.

Many of the books listed here are not myths or legends. These can be related to Sessions 2 through 6 of the GEMS unit, depending on their focus. *How to Dig a Hole to the Other Side of the World* works well with Session 2, in which students explore the concept of a ball-shaped Earth. Stories that include eclipses of the Moon or the Sun would fit well with Session 4, "Modeling Moon Phases and Eclipses." Any book about the Big Dipper enhances Session 5, in which students learn how to use the Big Dipper to tell time and to find the North Star. Books about other constellations relate best to Session 6, *Using Star Maps*.

Several books listed, such as those about comets or planets, are connected more generally to the subject of astronomy. Such books can be used to lead students from their investigations of the Earth, Moon and stars to other elements of our solar system. Books are listed alphabetically, by title.

Boat Ride With Lillian Two Blossom written and illustrated by Patricia Polacco. Philomel/Putnam & Grosset, New York. 1988. Grades: K–4.

A wise and mysterious Native American woman takes William and Mabel on a boat ride, starting in Michigan and ranging through the sky. Explanations for the rain, the wind, and the changing nature of the sky refer to spirits such as the caribou or polar bear which are magically shown.

Einstein Anderson Lights Up the Sky by Seymour Simon. Illustrated by Fred Winkowski. Viking Press, New York. 1982. Grades: 4–7.

In Chapter 2, "The World in His Hands," Einstein punctures his friend Stanley's plan to build a scale model of the solar system in his basement. He discusses the relative sizes of the Sun and the planets and the distances between them. In Chapter 5, "The Stars Like Grains of Sand," Einstein enlightens his younger brother Dennis about the star population.

Einstein Anderson Tells a Comet's Tale by Seymour Simon. Illustrated by Fred Winkowski. Viking Press, New York. 1981. Grades: 4–7.

Chapter 1, "Tale of the Comet," provides some very interesting information about possible connections between comets, asteroids, and dinosaurs. Even though the book was published in 1981, the information is accurate as of this writing.

Follow the Drinking Gourd written and illustrated by Jeanette Winter. Alfred A. Knopf, New York. 1988. Grades: K–6.

By following the hidden directions in the song, ""The Drinking Gourd," taught to them by an old sailor named Peg Leg Joe, runaway slaves follow the stars along the Underground Railroad and the connecting waterways to Canada and freedom. The "drinking gourd," another name for the Big Dipper, guided them north. In Sessions 5 and 6 of *Earth, Moon and Stars*, students learn how to use the Big Dipper to tell time and find the North Star.

Grandfather Twilight by Barbara Berger. Philomel Books/Putnam & Grosset, New York. 1984. Grades: Pre–2.

At the end of the day, as he does each day, Grandfather Twilight delivers the Moon to the sky. The Moon is a pearl which is removed from a strand and grows in size with each step grandfather takes. The story is portrayed simply, with few words and peaceful, yet magical illustrations.

How Many Stars in the Sky? by Lenny Hort. Illustrated by James E. Ransome. Tambourine Books/ William Morrow, New York. 1991. Grades: K–2.

An African-American father and son set off on a journey of discovery to count the stars in a summer night sky. As city-dwellers, they discover the obstacles to stargazing, city lights, for example, and end up driving to the country.

How to Dig a Hole to the Other Side of the World by Faith McNulty. Illustrated by Marc Simont. Harper Collins, New York. 1990. Grades: K–8.

A child takes an imaginary 8000-mile journey through the Earth and discovers what's inside. See page 62 for a more detailed version of how this activity connects beautifully with Session 2: Earth's Shape and Gravity.

In the Beginning: Creation Stories from Around the World by Virginia Hamilton. Illustrated by Barry Moser. Harcourt, Brace, Jovanovich, San Diego. 1988. Grades: All.

An illustrated collection of twenty-five legends explaining the creation of the world, with commentary placing the myth geographically and by type of myth tradition such as "world parent," "creation from nothing,"and "separation of earth and sky." Some of the selections are extracted from larger works such as the Popol Vuh or the Icelandic Eddas. In Session 1 of *Earth, Moon and Stars*, students learn several ways ancient peoples modeled how the Sun and Earth move.

Many Moons by James Thurber. Illustrated by Louis Slobodkin. Harcourt, Brace & World, New York. 1943. Grades: K–5.

This is the tale of a little princess who wanted the Moon, and of how she got it. Neither the King, the Lord High Chamberlain, the Royal Wizard, the Royal Mathematician, nor the Court Jester are able to solve the problem—it takes a 10-year old princess to figure it out. Includes a debate about how far away the Moon is.

Moon-Watch Summer by Lenore Blegvad. Illustrated by Erik Blegvad. Harcourt Brace Jovanovich, San Diego. 1972. Out-of-print. Grades: 4–6.

Adam's eager anticipation of the Apollo landing and first moonwalk turns to sullen resentment when he learns that he and his younger sister will be spending the summer on his grandmother's farm where there isn't even a television set. Once there, he is surprised when his grandmother confesses that she has always been "a sort of ancient moon-worshiper" fascinated by the Sea of Rainbows. He consoles himself with an old radio, hearing with frustration reports of good television transmission. "Mission Control called it a 'superb' quality picture. It had been seen 'live' in the United States, Japan, Western Europe, and South America. but not there in Grammie's house. Oh no, in Grammie's house there were 'so many other things to do,' who needed television?" As the summer progresses, he makes charts and drawings summarizing the mission's progress and learns to put his family responsibilities before personal disappointments. Today's students may find it hard to imagine life without television, but will appreciate the significance of the moonwalk to Adam and to society at that time. "On the Moon the astronauts were putting on their moon suits: the same fiber glass, nylon-plastic, double-layered thermal meteoroid garments, equipped with sockets for oxygen and water tubes and containing an incredibly complex communication system, that Adam had drawn the night before. All over the world, people gaped at their television screens, waiting to see the first human being step onto the Moon."

Nine O'Clock Lullaby by Marilyn Singer. Illustrated by Frane Lessac. HarperCollins, New York. 1991. Grades: Pre–6.

Bedtime story transports children through many lands showing what people might be doing on different parts of the globe at the "same" time. The pictures of the various cultures are fresh and lively from cooking on a "barbie" in Australia to conga drumming and coconut candy in Puerto Rico. On the last page, there's a brief astronomical explanation of time. This, and the idea that it is day on one part of the Earth while it is night on another part can be modeled for students in "Modeling Moon Phases," Activity 3 of the GEMS guide. This book could be read aloud to students even as old as the sixth grade to help make the concept real.

Planet of Exile by Ursula LeGuin. Ace Books, New York. 1966. Grades: 6–adult.

"Cooperation" is the central theme of this thin but gripping book about the clash of three cultures—two that have inhabited this harsh planet for eons, and the one that has been exiled only a few generations. Difficult seasonal conditions on the planet are the result of how long it takes for the planet to revolve once around its central star. Because one "year" is equivalent to many Earth years, people only live through a very small number of winters.

Quillworker: A Cheyenne Legend adapted by Terri Cohlene. Illustrated by Charles Reasoner. Watermill Press/Educational Reading Services, Mahwah, New Jersey. 1990. Grades: 2–5.

A Cheyenne legend that explains the origin of the Big Dipper constellation. Quillworker is an only child and an expert needleworker. Her dreams direct her to make seven buckskin warrior outfits for her mysterious new seven brothers. To escape the buffalo nation who want to take Quillworker, they all ride a tree up into the sky where they remain, with Quillworker as the brightest star in the dipper. In Session 5 of the GEMS guide, students study star clocks and the Big Dipper.

Sky Songs by Myra Cohn Livingston. Illustrated by Leonard E. Fisher. Holiday House, New York. 1984. Grades: 5–12.

Fourteen poems about various aspects of the sky such as the Moon, clouds, stars, storms, and sunsets. Wonderful images portray the planets as "wanderers of night," shooting stars are "bundled up in interstellar dust and bright icy jackets," and the morning sky is "earth's astrodome, floodlit."

Space Songs by Myra Cohn Livingston. Illustrated by Leonard E. Fisher. Holiday House, New York. 1988. Grades: 5–12.

Series of short poems about aspects of outer space including the Milky Way, Moon, Sun, stars, planets, comets, meteorites, asteroids, satellites and secrets. Although the astronomy content is limited, it is accurate. The black background illustrations are dynamic and involving.

Star Tales: North American Indian Stories retold and illustrated by Gretchen W. Mayo. Walker & Co., New York. 1987. Grades: 5–12.

The nine legends in this collection explain observations of the stars, Moon, and night sky. Accompanying each tale is information about the constellation or other heavenly observation and how various tribes perceived it. In More Star Tales, the author includes "The Never-Ending Bear Hunt" and seven other tales.

The Heavenly Zoo, Legends and Tales of the Stars by Alison Lurie. Illustrated by Monika Beisner. Farrar Straus & Giroux, New York. 1979. Originally published in Germany. Grades: 4–8.

A collection of 16 tales from all over the world retold by a well-known author. "Long before anyone knew that the stars were great burning globes of gas many millions of miles from the Earth and from one another, men and women saw the sky filled with magical pictures outlined with points of light. Some of these tales are heroic, some comic, some sad; but all are full of wonder we still feel when we look at the sky full of stars." The illustrations are striking, showing each beast, bird, or fish against the stars that indicate its position.

The Magic School Bus Lost in the Solar System by Joanna Cole. Illustrated by Bruce Degen. Scholastic Inc., New York. 1990. Grades: K–6.

Ms. Frizzle and her class leave the Earth and visit the Moon, Sun, and each planet in the Solar System, noting the temperature, color, size, and unique features. Perfect for students who want to extend their investigations in the *Earth, Moon and Stars* unit to a study of the Solar System.

The Planet of Junior Brown by Virginia Hamilton. Macmillan Publishing, New York. 1971. Grades: 5–12.

This unusual and moving book begins with three people (two students who regularly cut 8th grade classes and a school custodian who was formerly a teacher) in a secret room in a school basement with a working model of the solar system. The model has one incredible addition — a giant planet named for one of the students, Junior Brown. How can the Earth's orbit not be affected by this giant planet? Is there a belt of asteroids that balances it all out? How does this relate to equilateral triangles? From these subjects, the universe of the book expands outward into the Manhattan streets and inward into the hearts, minds, and friendship of the two students who are both African-American. Buddy Clark is a streetwise, homeless, extremely intelligent and resourceful young man who helps younger homeless boys as part of an elaborate system of hideouts and support, where each base is also called a "planet." Junior Brown, artistically and musically talented, but very overweight, is plagued by family crisis, lack of self-esteem, delusions, and eventually severe psychiatric disturbance. After the first chapter, the solar system becomes more metaphor than scientific model, until the end of the book when the real model must be dismantled and the three must find a way to help Junior Brown and to affirm their solidarity against all odds. Powerfully and poetically written, this book humanizes the statistics about homelessness and the educational crisis in a profound and unforgettable way.

The Planets edited by Byron Preiss. Bantam Books, New York. 1985. Grades: 8–adult.

This extremely rich, high-quality anthology pairs a non-fiction essay with a fictional work about the Earth, Moon, each of the planets, and asteroids and comets; with introductory essays by Asimov, Clarke and others. Written by respected authors and scientists, the material is dazzlingly illustrated with color photographs from the archives of NASA and the Jet Propulsion Laboratory, and paintings by astronomical artists such as the production designers of 2001 and Star Wars. The story "Handprints on the Moon" by William K. Hartmann tells of two male scientists who are on the Moon as part of a U.S. mission. From the vehicle rolling across the plains of the Moon, the author describes the lunar surface and remembers nights of gazing through a telescope in Illinois. They meet up with a group of Russian scientists led by Valentina Levin, a biochemist. Her project is monitoring lava tubes for emissions of gases. An interesting fantasy is the Neolithic cave style lava wall that bears the handprints, the "signatures," of every human who has been on the Moon.

The Truth about the Moon by Clayton Bess. Illustrated by Rosekrans Hoffman. Houghton Mifflin Co., Boston. 1983. Grades: K–4.

Tale about an African boy named Sumu who is puzzled by the changing size of the Moon and asks for an explanation. His father says there is only one moon and that the moon he saw last night is the same moon he will see tomorrow. "It is growing, just as a child like you grows to be a man like me. It starts small, just a silver sliver, and every night grows bigger and bigger until it is as big as it can be, a full circle. Then, just as a man grows smaller when he is very old, so does the moon. Smaller and smaller until death." His mother explains that there is only one moon. "It is like a woman. And you know how sometimes a woman will grow larger and larger, more and more round?" The Chief tells a long tale about the Sun and the Moon being married and how the Moon lost its heat.

The Way To Start a Day by Byrd Baylor. Illustrated by Peter Parnall. Charles Scribner's Sons, New York. 1978. Macmillan Publishing Co., New York. 1986. Grades: 3–7.

Gives examples of the ways that peoples of the world have celebrated the dawn with drum beats, ringing of bells, gifts of gold or flowers. "The way to start the day is this — Go outside and face the east and greet the Sun with some kind of blessing or chant or song that you made yourself and keep for early morning." Relates to Session 1 of the GEMS guide. Caldecott honor book.

The Year of The Comet by Roberta Wiegand. Bradbury Press, Scarsdale, New York. 1984. Out-of-print. Age: 4–9.

This book is a very sensitive and well-described portrait of Sarah, born in 1900, who has always lived in a small town in Nebraska. It takes place in 1910, the year of the re-arrival to Earth view of Halley's Comet. The first two chapters are specifically about the comet, the rumors about massive destruction that preceded it, and its actual impact on the community. These chapters could stand alone as a literary extension to *Earth, Moon, and Stars*. The second chapter also starts with an interesting narrative involving the theme of scale, as Sarah puts herself, like Alice going down the rabbit hole, inside a map of the U.S. to delve into the detail of the buildings and streets of her small town. For many students, it will be hard not to continue reading of Sarah's other adventures as she gains a new maturity during "the year of the comet." Many touching and powerful passages; a good sense of the universal scope of the comet and the real-life complexity of human relations.

To Space and Back by Sally Ride with Susan Okie. Lothrop, Lee and Shepard/Morrow, New York. 1986. Grades: 4–7.

What it is like to travel in space — to live, sleep, eat, and work in conditions unlike anything we know on Earth, told in Ride's own words and through colored photographs aboard ship and in space. She talks about the scientific experiments they conduct observing and photographing the stars and the Earth and other planets and galaxies. Working outside the shuttle, they feel the warmth of the Sun through their gloves but cool off on the dark side of Earth in the shade. This, and other descriptions, could lead to a better understanding of the Earth's shape and gravity (Session 2 of the GEMS guide) as well as day/night and phases of the Moon.

As this guide was revised in 1996, we received a recommendation of two more books as possible literature connections to this unit:

*Moontellers—
Myths of the Moon From Around the World*
by Lynn Moroney
Northland Publishing
Flagstaff, Arizona, 1995.

How We Learned the Earth Is Round
by Patricia Lauber; illustrator, Megan Lloyd
Thomas Y. Crowell, New York, 1990.
(Designed for younger students, this book explores humanity's varying theories about the shape of the Earth.)

DIGGING A HOLE

In Session 2 of the GEMS unit *Earth, Moon, and Stars*, students grapple with the concepts of the Earth's shape and gravity. They apply their mental models of the Earth to real and imaginary situations as they engage in animated discussions. One of the discussion questions asks students to pretend that a tunnel was dug all the way through the Earth, from pole to pole. Students are asked to imagine that a person holds a rock above the opening at the North Pole, and then drops the rock into the tunnel. What happens to the rock?

While this age-old question is used to stretch students to apply their understanding of the concept of gravity, many a class has enjoyed thinking and talking about the tunnel itself and what the center of the Earth is like.

How to Dig a Hole to the Other Side of the World by Faith McNulty, (HarperCollins Publishers, 1979) is a wonderful children's literature book that can capitalize on your students' curiosity about the center of the Earth. This clever book provides instructions for those who want to dig to the other side of the world. Beginning with:

"Find a soft place. Take a shovel and start to dig a hole. The dirt you dig up is called loam. Loam, or topsoil, is made up of tiny bits of rock mixed with many other things, such as plants and worms that died and rotted long ago."

The digging goes on, through the next layer of clay, gravel, or sand, through rockier soil, to bedrock. But it doesn't stop there! Diggers are instructed on how to get through bedrock, through the water table, through magma, the mantle, the outer core, the inner core, to the center of the Earth. And that's only halfway through the Earth!

The book has practical tips for the diggers, about using a bucket to pull up the soil and rocks as you go, about using a drill when you come to bedrock, an underwater diving suit for when you hit underground rivers and lakes, and yes, a jet-propelled submarine with a super cooling system, a fireproof skin and a drill at the tip of its nose for negotiating through the magma. It warns you to watch out for fossils, diamonds, geysers (that could deliver you suddenly back to the surface), gooey oil deposits, and more. It gives the following advice for when you reach the center of the Earth:

"At the center of the Earth there is nothing under you. Every direction is up. Your feet are pointing up and your head is pointing up, both at the same time. Because there is nothing under you, you will weigh nothing...The weight of the whole world will press down on your ship. Do not stay long."

The final surprise is that you don't end up in China, but at the bottom of the Indian Ocean (if you left from the United States, that is). This delightful 8000 mile journey through the Earth provides students with information in the most vivid way. It is an ideal use of children's literature to extend the science investigations begun in *Earth, Moon, and Stars*.

Assessment Suggestions

Selected Student Outcomes

1. Students are able to make systematic observations of the sky and create models to explain their observations.

2. Students are able to reconcile what they have been told about the Earth's spherical shape with its flat appearance.

3. Students are able to apply the concept of gravity to explain what happens to people and objects on or inside the Earth.

4. Students use a concrete model of the Earth, Moon, and Sun to explain phases of the moon and eclipses.

5. Students locate constellations in the night sky; describe how they move during the evening; and explain this movement in terms of the rotation of the Earth on its axis.

6. Students pose and answer some of their own questions about the Earth, Moon, and stars.

Built-In Assessment Activities

What Are Your Students' Ideas?

To find out students preconceptions about the Earth, Sun, stars, and Moon, questions are suggested at the beginning of most activities. For example, in Session 3 they are asked to describe phases of the moon, and to explain why phases occur. (Outcome 1, 4)

Questionnaire About the Earth's Shape and Gravity

In Session 2, students are asked to fill out a questionnaire about the Earth's shape and gravity. Collect the papers after individual students have completed them, before they are allowed to discuss their ideas with others. The students then discuss those concepts in small and large groups. After the unit is completed, give the questionnaire again, to see how much students have learned. (Outcomes 2, 3)

Note: This activity is a featured case study with student work in Insights and Outcome: Assessments for Great Explorations in Math and Science, the GEMS assessment handbook. The handbook includes selected student learning outcomes for all GEMS teacher's guides.

Setting Your Star Clock Alarm

In Session 5, students create a Star Clock and find out how to use it. To assess their understanding, use a large cardboard version of a Star Clock. Ask your students to set their Star Clocks for a specific time, such as 6:00 a.m., and to note the positions of the stars at that time. Then move the hands of the large clock in front of the class, and ask students to make a ringing noise when the stars have reached the position that they will have at the preset time. (Outcome 5)

Assessment Suggestions *(continued)*

Additional Assessment Ideas

Predictions

After the unit is completed, when the moon is visible in the sky, ask your students to predict where it will be the next day or the next week. When the moon is not visible, ask: "Where is the Moon now?" "Why can't we see it?" This will reveal the knowledge students retain and can apply beyond the duration of the unit. (Outcomes 1, 4)

Letter Writing

Ask your students to write a letter to a younger student explaining why people think the Earth is really round, even though it looks flat; or why the moon goes through different phases. You will gain information about the accuracy of students' conclusions as well as their ability to clearly communicate what they know. (Outcome 2)

What Do You Wonder?

Have your students work in small groups to brainstorm further questions they have about the Earth, Moon, and stars. Discuss their ideas about possible answers to these questions. (Outcome 6)

Summary Outlines

Activity 1: Ancient Models of the World

Getting Ready

Make one copy of activity sheet for each student.

Part I. Models of the World

1. Ask students to describe daily motion of Sun.
2. Ask how Sun gets from west to east during the night.
3. Introduce model as a person's explanation for something observed.
4. Hand out copies of "Ancient Models of the World." Tell students they would have been taught one of these models in school, 3,000 years ago.
5. Ask for volunteers to read explanations for each model. Discuss different explanations for each phenomena, and how they reflect the surroundings of the different cultures.
6. Challenge students to invent models of the world to explain Sun's daily motion.
7. Organize students into pairs and hand out scratch paper.
8. Give each pair of students a large sheet of white paper and colors.
9. Ask students to think about how they will describe their models to classmates.

Part II. Presentations

1. Pairs of students discuss ideas. Discuss each idea.
2. Summarize lesson by showing that many models can explain same observations.
3. End with additional information on history of astronomy:
   a. Greece was center of trade routes, exchanged stories.
   b. By Columbus in 1492, people believed in ball-shaped Earth, but disagreed about side of the ball.

Activity 2. The Earth's Shape and Gravity

Getting Ready

1. Make one copy of questionnaire for each student, plus 8 extras.
2. Borrow 8 earth globes or other balls and stands.

Part I. What Are Your Ideas?

1. Students fill out questionnaires. Collect papers.
2. Organize discussion groups.
3. Give each group a globe and blank questionnaire.
4. Circulate and encourage students to demonstrate ideas to each other.

Part II. Discussion

1. Play role of moderator of discussion about answers to questions.
2. Poll students on answers. Do not announce correct answers!
3. Correct answers are:

> Question 1: d.
> Question 2: d.
> Question 3: rocks fall straight down to feet of person who dropped them.
> Question 4: either rock falls to center of Earth and stops (simple understanding of gravity), or rock oscillates in the tunnel (more sophisticated under standing of gravity).

4. After discussion, give correct answers as answers that most scientists give.
5. You may want to give questionnaire 2 or 3 weeks later as evaluation.

Activity 3: Observing the Moon

Getting Ready

1. Just before class, go outdoors and find Moon.
2. Have paper, pencils, and manila folders on hand.

Part I. Measuring in Fists

1. Ask if students saw Moon that morning and what it looked like.
2. Explain that students will start observing Moon for 1 month.
3. Hand out paper, pencils, folders, and go outdoors to observe Moon.
4. Gather students where they can see the Moon. Ask which side faces toward or away from Sun.
5. Ask students to draw Sun and Moon; put names and dates on paper.
6. Demonstrate how to measure in "fists."
7. Ask students to measure distance between Sun and Moon in fists.
8. Tell students to write number of fists on paper.

Part II. Observing the Moon

1. Have students observe/record Moon's distance from the Sun every other day.
2. Discuss how Moon changes shape and distance after each observation.
3. Give names of phases: gibbous, quarter (or half), crescent, new, and full.

Part III: Summarizing the Data

1. Summarize observations after about ten days.
2. On large sheet of butcher paper, draw Sun. Average number of fists between Sun and Moon on first observation date.
3. With marker, draw Sun and Moon on each date observed. Write date and number of fists from Sun under each picture of Moon.
4. Ask students to describe pattern.
5. Ask: "Where is the Moon now? Why can't we see it anymore? When will we be able to see it? Where will it be?"
6. Go to next activity, even if students have difficulty with above questions.
7. Assign students to start observing Moon each night in the evening.

Activity 4: Modeling Moon Phases and Eclipses

Getting Ready

1. Find room that can be darkened completely.
2. Plug in lamp and place in middle of room, about eye level.
3. Have polystyrene balls, or styrofoam balls painted with white opaque paint.
4. Try out different bulbs to see which is best.

Part I. Model Earth, Moon, and Sun

1. Review results of Moon observations.
2. Remind students of meaning of "model."
3. Tell students about Egyptians' ideas of why Moon has phases.
4. 2,000 years ago the Greeks thought of a model of Moon that we believe today. Darken room, with only lamp in center giving illumination.
5. Arrange students in circle around lamp.
6. Hand out moon balls. Have students push balls onto pencil points as "handles."
7. Explain that heads represent Earth, light represents Sun, and white ball represents the moon.

Part II: Observing Moon Phases

1. Ask students to hold ball at arm's length, directly in front of sun.
2. Tell students to move ball to left until they see a thin crescent.
3. Look around room and help as needed.
4. Ask if bright side of moon is facing toward or away from sun.
5. Continue moving moon to left until half is lit. Ask: "For moon to be fuller, does it have to move towards or away from sun?"
6. Continue moving moon until fully lit. Move above the shadow of your heads.
7. Keep moving moon in circle until half full again. Ask: "As moon moves towards sun, does it get fuller or thinner?"
8. Continue moving moon in same direction until a thin crescent (new moon).
9. Move moon in circle several times to learn pattern of phases.

Part III. Observing Eclipses

1. Move moon directly in front of sun to form solar eclipse.
2. Notice shadow on everyone's eyes. Only people under shadow can see eclipse.
3. Move moon in circle until full phase. Pass into shadow of your head.
4. This is an eclipse of the moon. Ask, "Can you see shape of your head?"
5. Ask, "Can everyone who lives on your face see the eclipse? Can people on the back of your head see it? "
6. Continue moving moon until near solar eclipse. What phase is it in? What phase is it in just before eclipse of the moon?
7. Review solar and lunar eclipses.

Activity 5: Making a Star Clock

Getting Ready

1. Make one copy of the Instruction Sheet for each student and one for yourself.
2. Make one star clock.
3. Make a star clock poster.
4. Tape poster to the wall in the 7PM position.

Part I. Making Star Clocks

1. Ask how people could tell time before clocks were invented.
2. Give instruction sheet, paper fastener, and scissors to each student.
3. Explain how to cut out circles and notch in one circle.
4. Demonstrate how to insert fastener.

Part II. Using Star Clocks in Class

1. Focus attention on poster.
2. Define constellations. Point out constellations on the poster.
3. Ask if students have seen these constellations at night.
4. Tell students to find current month around outside of star clock. Put thumb on current date and hold so current date is up.
5. Turn inner circle so stars line up as they appear in the sky. Point out imaginary line formed by stars in bowl of dipper.
6. Read time in window.
7. Ask students for times they read. Help as needed.
8. Illustrate how stars turn during night by rotating poster. Ask students to read time again.
9. Tell students to "set their alarm clocks at 6AM and to ring when that time arrives. Rotate poster and stop when students "ring"!
10. Assign use of star clock at night, comparing with watch.
11. Tell students to use clocks when stars first come out, and just before they go to bed.

Part III. A Spinning Earth

1. Ask students how star clocks worked.
2. Explain long ago people thought the stars were little bits of light. Today we know they are huge suns.
3. Have students stand, point overhead and turn.
4. Ask students where North Star is in the model.

Activity 6: Using Star Maps

Getting Ready

1. Select current star map and find constellations yourself.
2. Make three posters in addition to the one from the previous activity.
3. Tape posters to walls of classroom. Use front of classroom as north.
4. Make one copy of current star map for each student.

Part I: Making Star Maps

1. Discuss constellations on the poster in front of the room.
2. Imagine Big Dipper as a Big Bear.
3. Explain how to find directions with Big Dipper and North Star.
4. Give students star maps.
5. Explain how to use star map:
    a. Find constellation on map.
    b. Is it near horizon or zenith?
    c. What direction do you face?
    d. Use North Star to find direction.
    e. Hold map so direction you face is down, on bottom of page.
6. Challenge students to find other constellation posters in room.
7. Invite students to take maps home and find constellations in night sky.

Part II. Changing Stars.

1. Ask students about their experiences finding constellations.
2. Find constellations when stars first come out.
3. Find same constellations again just before going to bed. How did constellations move?
4. Recall how stars moved in star clocks activity.

Part III. Spinning Earth Revisited

1. Ask students how they observed stars moving.
2. Have students stand and turn, this time staring straight ahead. They will see objects (stars) move into view (rise), while others pass out of view (set).
3. Turn again, looking up, noticing how stars move near the North Star.

Ancient Models of the World

In each of the countries listed on this page, there were many different stories about the world. Here are just a few of those stories.

EGYPT

The Earth is flat. The sky is like a flat plate, supported at four places by mountains. The sun is carried across the sky in a boat, from east to west. At night, the sun is carried back to the east through the Underworld.

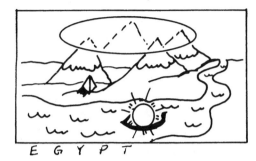

INDIA

The Earth is a circular disk, surrounded by the ocean. In the center of the world is a great mountain. The sun goes around the mountain once a day. In the evening, the sun goes behind the western side of the mountain. It travels behind the mountain at night, and comes out on the eastern side in the morning.

CHINA

The sky is a round dome, surrounding a flat square-shaped Earth. The ocean goes all around the Earth. The sun travels in a big tilted circle. At night the sun is not under the Earth, but rather on the side of the Earth.

GREECE

Most ancient Greeks believed that the Earth floated in the ocean like a cork in water. One person, named Anaximander, thought that the Earth was a cylinder with a rounded top, floating in the air. The sky surrounded the Earth, and beyond the sky was a region of fire. The sun, moon, and stars were holes in the sky, through which the fire could be seen.

Name_____ Date_____

WHAT ARE YOUR IDEAS ABOUT THE EARTH?

QUESTION 1: Why is the Earth flat in picture #1 and round in picture #2?
(Circle the letter in front of the best answer.)

 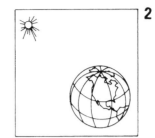

A. They are different Earths.

B. The Earth is round like a ball, but people live on the flat part in the middle.

C. The Earth is round like a ball, but it has flat spots on it.

D. The Earth is round like a ball but looks flat because we see only a small part of the ball.

E. The Earth is round like a plate or record, so it seems round when you're over it and flat when you're on it.

QUESTION 2: Pretend that the Earth is glass and you can look through it. **Which way would you look, in a straight line, to see people in far-off countries like China or India?**

A. Westward? **B.** Eastward? **C.** Upward? **D.** Downward?

QUESTION 3: This drawing shows some enlarged people dropping rocks at various places around the Earth. **Show what happens to each rock by drawing a line showing the complete path of the rock, from the person's hand to where it finally stops.**

Why will the rock fall that way?

QUESTION 4: Pretend that a tunnel was dug all the way through the Earth, from pole to pole. Imagine that a person holds a rock above the opening at the North Pole, and drops it. **Draw a line from the person's hand showing the entire path of the rock.**

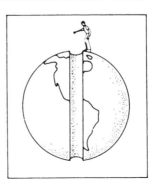

Why will the rock fall that way?

Modified and adapted from the February issue of *Learning 86*, copyright 1986, Springhouse Corporation.

Great Explorations in Math and Science: *Earth, Moon, and Stars*

Instruction Sheet:
How to Make and Use a Star Clock

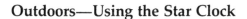

Indoors—Making the Star Clock

1. Cut out the two circles with a pair of scissors.

2. Cut out the notch on the small circle.

3. Use a paper punch to make a hole in the center of the small circle.

4. Place the small circle on top of the large circle. Push a large paper fastener down through the center of both circles, and spread open the fastener on the back side of the Star Clock.

Outdoors—Using the Star Clock

1. Find the Big Dipper and the North Star, as shown on the face of your Star Clock.

2. Face the North Star, as shown on the front of the clock.

3. Find the current month around the outside circle of the Star Clock. Put your thumb over the current month. Hold your Star Clock so the current month, marked by your thumb, is AT THE TOP.

4. Holding the large disk firmly with the current date at the top, turn the smaller disk until its stars line up with those in the sky.

5. Read the time in the window.

6. If you are on Daylight Savings Time, add one hour.

© 1986 by the Regents of the University of California
Great Explorations in Math and Science: *Earth, Moon, and Stars*

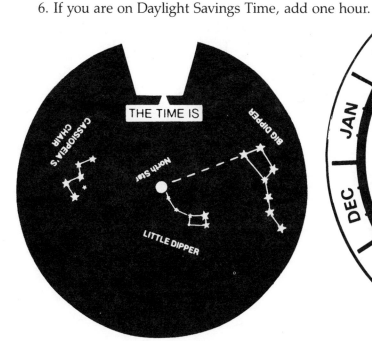

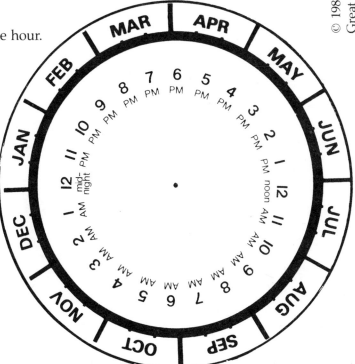

Notes

Notes

Notes